Lindal Living

DISCOVERING YOUR DREAM

Every custom
home begins with
a dream.
WHAT'S YOURS?
CONRAD RESIDENCE, CA. CUSTOM HOME.

CARROLL RESIDENCE, MT. CUSTOMIZED SUMMIT.

Bringing it to life is
our specialty.
FOR MORE THAN HALF
A CENTURY.

We create the
best of plans:
yours alone.

NO WONDER IT FEELS LIKE HOME.

CUSTOM RESIDENCE, CA. DREAM RANCH PLAN.

O'BRIEN RESIDENCE, CA. PROW STAR: VIEWVISTA PLAN ® 85

We build legendary
style & quality
into every square foot.
WHY COMPROMISE?

We craft your dream with the most beautiful building material

on earth.

THE FINEST WESTERN RED CEDAR IS YOURS.

BOYLE RESIDENCE, VA. LAKEFRONT LIVING PLAN Ⓛ 105.

BOYLE

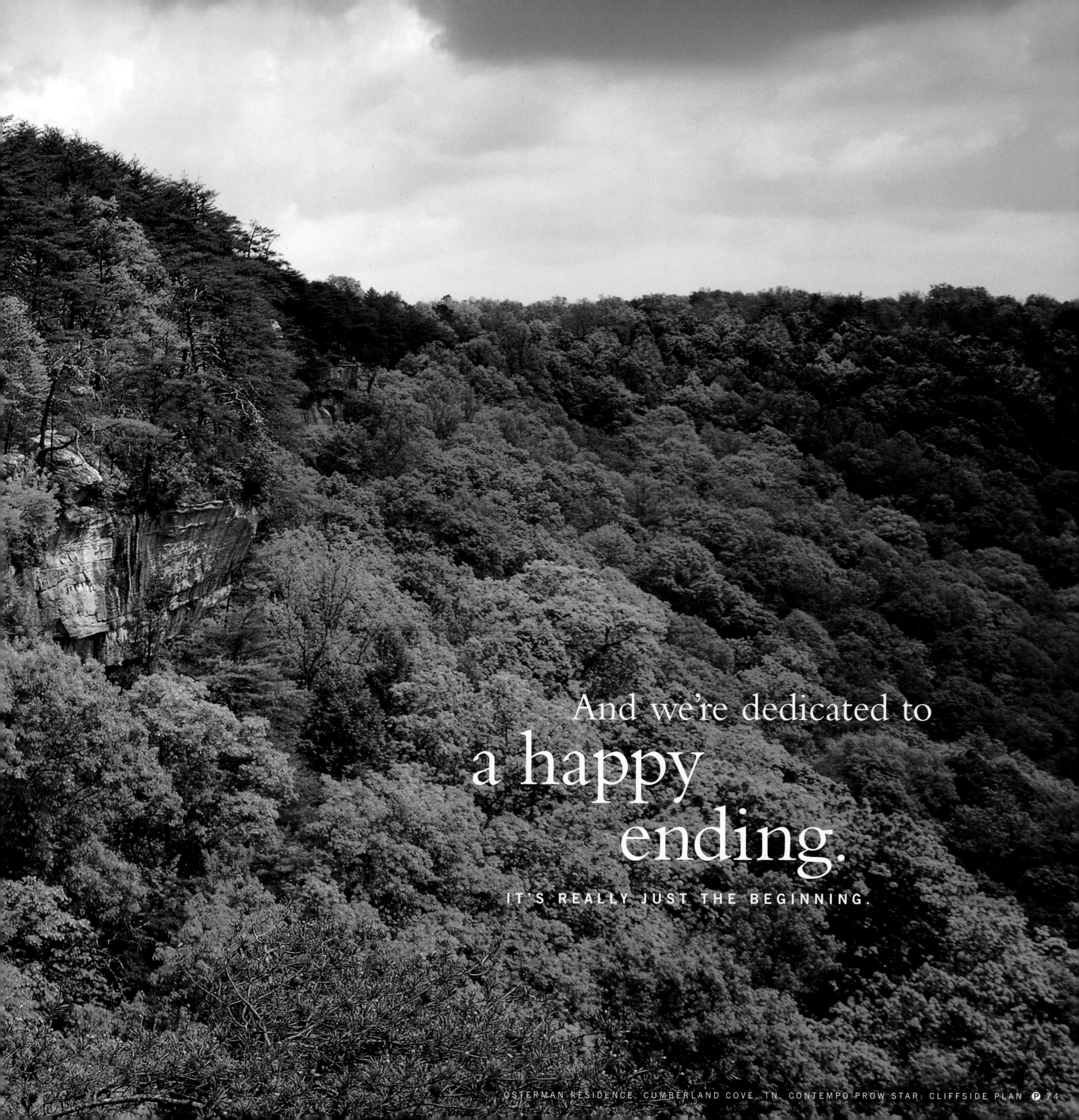

And we're dedicated to
a happy
ending.
IT'S REALLY JUST THE BEGINNING.

OSTERMAN RESIDENCE, CUMBERLAND COVE, TN. CONTEMPO PROW STAR: CLIFFSIDE PLAN P 74.

CARMICHAEL RESIDENCE, WA. CUSTOMIZED PROW STAR

Welcome to
Lindal Living.
BRINGING YOUR WAY OF LIFE HOME.

LORIMER RESIDENCE, CA. COASTAL CONTEMPORARY PLAN Ⓛ 67.

CONTENTS

Many photographs and floorplans are cross-referenced in Lindal Living **L** *or Lindal Planning* **P**.

How can you ensure that the custom home of your dreams is the home you'll get? Today's tremendous variations in the quality of building design and materials make it more important than ever to know what you're getting for your money. And there are some secrets to success that are difficult to put a price on — like the value of having a custom home expert as your close personal advisor and advocate in bringing your vision to life. At Lindal, we're proud to present the people, the process and the legendary materials behind our longstanding reputation for beauty. Structural integrity. Low maintenance. And lasting value on a wide range of budgets. Here's how the Lindal difference makes a difference to you.

Your Vision

"MOST GUESTS THINK 'CABIN' BEFORE THEY VISIT. THEY LEAVE THINKING 'CATHEDRAL!'"

— *Bob & Marilyn Van Wagner, Yacolt, Washington*

Your pleasures. Your priorities. Your personal sense of comfort and style. At Lindal, design consultation is an integral part of planning your new home. Chances are you'll find the custom home of your dreams in Lindal's extensive and exclusive collection of architectural styles, home sizes and floorplans. Whether you want to move a window, enlarge a room, or change the exterior style of your home, count on your local Lindal dealer and Lindal's Design Department to make the necessary modifications to your favorite plan. Together, they can create your home design, whether it's from a napkin sketch or your architect's blueprint, making a Lindal of lasting structural integrity and enduring quality — guaranteed.

YOUR STYLE

Is your dream home a Classic Lindal with lofty ceilings and spectacular views? A Tudor with the storybook charm of the English countryside? A timeless American farmhouse that has the character of small towns and wide-open spaces? Ask yourself what architectural style speaks to you; you'll find the answer in a Lindal. And, should you choose to work with your own architect, you'll appreciate how much your Lindal dealer will contribute to the process.

YOUR SIZE

Lindal design makes the best and most beautiful use of every square foot, whether you choose to build a small treasure or live on a grand scale. There's an art to aligning a home's style and size to create a sense of proportion that's a pleasure to live in. You know it when you see it, and you see it in Lindal design.

YOUR SITE

Lindal design can enhance the lay of your land. Make the most of a view. Build privacy into a small city lot. Triumph over a sloping site. And make your house at home in its natural environment.

YOUR CLIMATE

Lindals are at home anywhere — come rain, shine or other climatic extremes. We design and engineer homes to meet the most demanding snow, wind and seismic requirements. In the tropics, Lindal homes combat heat, humidity, insects and pests — and welcome trade winds. Your local dealer can help you address any special considerations to the challenges of your climate.

YOUR PRIORITIES

A growing number of homeowners are delighted to discover that a Lindal is well within their budget. Whether you're starting out, scaling down or moving up, we deliver on our promise to provide the finest home money can buy, across a wide range of prices. When you figure in the lifetime low maintenance and energy efficiency of a Lindal, the bottom line is even more attractive.

PREVIOUS SPREAD No ordinary log home: This solid cedar Lindal combines contemporary design with the finest materials. Custom residence, WA. Enlightened Log Home Plan Ⓟ 108. **THIS PAGE** This Lindal was created for its own island. Gluek residence, Ontario. Customized Prow Star. **OPPOSITE:** 1. Stone accents the cedar exterior of a Classic Lindal with a view. Gilman residence, CA. Customized Contempo Prow Star. 2. Gabled dormers and a generous front porch are among the many charms of this Lindal Traditional. Custom residence, NY. Chapel Hill Plan Ⓟ 93. 3. The street appeal of this Lindal Contemporary is enhanced by a covered entry, a mix of roof heights and window shapes, and the light-gray vertical cedar siding. Hodgkinson residence, Ontario. Customized Ellington Plan Ⓟ 107.

3

BLINDSIGHT Robin Cook
Facing the Lions

Engineered for Life

"WE REFER TO OUR HOME AS BEING BUILT LIKE THE ROCK OF GIBRALTAR."

— *Stanley & Lois Grant, Manchester, New Hampshire*

The open, airy look that many Lindal homeowners love is more than a matter of style. It's the beauty of Lindal's exclusive engineered building system, inspired by the post and beam architecture of North American master builders. Our engineered post and beam building system generally frees up the interior walls from serving as structural supports, creating an interior that allows long spans, large expanses of glass — and the ability to easily customize a floorplan to your functional and aesthetic tastes. Lindal's signature engineering is our deepest expression of quality — the heart of creating homes as strong as they are beautiful.

DESIGN FREEDOM

Lindal engineering gives you the design flexibility dreams are made of. By freeing most interior walls from bearing any structural load, post and beam construction allows for a floorplan that can be fine-tuned to the way you live. It supports a free-flowing sense of expansiveness that welcomes soaring ceilings. A graceful flow of living spaces. Walls of windows. And a room filled with natural light.

In addition to our classic post and beam building system, Lindal offers an alternate framing system — a system similar to that used by many residential builders. Most home designs can be built with either system, or a combination of the two — the choice is yours, and your local Lindal dealer can help you decide. Both Lindal building systems are engineered to guarantee the same enduring quality and value that have distinguished Lindal homes for generations.

UNDERLYING STRENGTHS

Lindal engineering gives your home a framework — with inner strength and structural integrity that often exceed local building practices. The difference is one you'll appreciate from the first day you live in your Lindal — and many years down the road, too. Because every aspect of a Lindal home is engineered to last.

Consider our standard Lindal Floor System — just one example of the many ways we engineer exceptional performance into every square foot. Lindal floors are strong, stable and virtually immune to the squeaks and bounces of so many floors today, adding daily comfort, low maintenance and high long-term value to your home. Dozens of other Lindal-engineered details make a difference, too. When it comes to building your dream, Lindal engineering is not only a good investment. It's a good feeling.

LINDAL ENGINEERING PAYS

Lindal engineering helps prevent costs from ballooning during construction. By pre-engineering and using high quality building materials, we craft reliability into every home. And we list all materials to let you know what your home will cost before it arrives on site.

Our thorough understanding of builders' needs eliminates many of the unknowns that typically cause surprises and drive up costs. The bottom line: Construction can proceed more smoothly and on schedule.

EASY EXPANSION

The ability to expand your home, with fewer structural constraints, is another strength of Lindal's classic post and beam engineering. As your needs grow and change, it's easy to take out interior walls or add a wing.

EXCLUSIVELY LINDAL

The innovations that distinguish the building system and structural integrity of your Lindal home are a result of an impressive array of U.S. and Canadian international patents — held by company founder and industry innovator, Sir Walter Lindal. So although Lindal homes are often imitated, nothing measures up to the original.

OPPOSITE Lindal engineering allows homeowners to make all kinds of design statements that are "outside the box." In the Gassners' Oregon Coast home, special Lindal engineering supports the octagonal design of their living room with its massive beams and cedar-lined ceiling. The cedar has been pickled to lighten the overall effect. Gassner residence, OR. Octagon Oasis Plan Ⓟ 110.

Your Personal Guide

"OUR LINDAL DEALERS WERE MORE THAN HELPFUL. THEIR SUPPORT, ADVICE, COMMUNICATION AND FRIENDSHIP MADE IT AN EXCITING AND JOYFUL TIME, ESPECIALLY SINCE WE WERE 500 MILES FROM THE SITE."

— *Don & Carole Forbes, Penhook, Virginia*

The best custom homes don't happen by chance; they take careful planning, knowledge, coordination and attention to detail. That's why one of the single biggest advantages of building a Lindal home is your local Lindal dealer. Your dealer is your personal guide to creating your custom home — providing expertise and insight every step of the way. In the process, you'll enjoy the high level of attentive service and home-planning knowledge it takes to bring a dream to life. Once you've discovered the difference this level of knowledgeable service makes, you'll wonder how you ever did without it — and why.

ABOVE/OPPOSITE The service and support of your local Lindal dealer make a difference throughout every step of the planning process, and in the long-term satisfaction with your home. Lindal homeowners appreciate that they can be involved in the planning process as much or as little as they like.

A VALUABLE RESOURCE

According to many Lindal homeowners, their dealer provided the missing link in the typical home-planning process — offering a level of personal assistance, planning and coordination they couldn't find anywhere else.

A DIFFERENCE FROM START TO FINISH

Your dealer can help you make the most of your site. Provide experienced, insightful design assistance. Analyze your plan's feasibility and cost. Refer you to experienced local builders of Lindal homes. And oversee your order through delivery — and beyond. Every step of the way, you can count on your dealer for the helpful tips and hands-on advice that elevate the value, beauty and livability of your home.

MASTERS OF PLANNING

With your dealer's help, you can be personally involved in planning your home as much or as little as you wish. Whether your dream home is an image in your head, an award-winning Lindal design, a sketch on a napkin, or your architect's design, you can count on your dealer to transform it into the best of plans.

LINDAL EXPERTISE

Lindal dealers bring you the advantages of all the design, planning and engineering resources Lindal has to offer — eliminating the risks and maximizing the rewards of creating your dream home.

LOCAL KNOW-HOW

With more than 150 independent Lindal dealers throughout North America and beyond, the home planning assistance you need is close at hand. So is your dealer's knowledge of local building codes and land-use issues, climatic considerations and financing options.

PERSONAL FOLLOW-THROUGH

In addition to working one-to-one with you, your dealer is in close contact with Lindal headquarters, coordinating everything from final design and blueprints to materials delivery. At Lindal, we believe you shouldn't have to put your life on hold while your home is being built.

Lindal
Lindal
CEDAR HOMES

The Material Difference

"WITH BOTH OF US BEING IN CONSTRUCTION ALL OF OUR LIVES, WE WERE EXTREMELY IMPRESSED WITH THE QUALITY OF MATERIALS IN OUR NEW LINDAL HOME. IT IS MOST DEFINITELY THE SHOWPLACE OF CENTRAL FLORIDA."

— *Les & Judy Patzer, Mulberry, Florida*

At Lindal, we've reserved nature's most perfect building material for you: a kiln-dried premium grade of Western red cedar you simply won't find anywhere else. In addition to superior cedar and building systems, an entire houseful of premium, above-grade materials are the secret to Lindal's dramatic beauty, structural integrity, low maintenance and living comfort. They all add up to lasting value. Homeowners say Lindal materials bring out the best in a construction crew, too.

DAILY LUXURY, LIFETIME BEAUTY

The natural wonders of Lindal's fragrant, fine-grained cedar come through in its radiance, warm range of colors and velvety finish — all of which make it a daily pleasure to live with. More than one homeowner has said that living in a home crafted of Lindal cedar is like being surrounded by a work of art. Others say the fragrance and radiance of the wood add a dimension of serenity and spirit to daily living.

LASTING STRENGTHS

The beauty of Lindal cedar is more than skin deep. Pound for pound, it's as strong as steel. Its natural preservative oils account for its durability and resistance to moisture, decay and insects. The bottom line: a lifetime of low maintenance and high value.

QUALITY CONTROL COUNTS

The extraordinary quality of Lindal cedar can't be matched at the local lumberyard. That's because we have our own high standards for the cedar that goes into every Lindal home. From the forest to the building site, our strict quality control standards and grading systems begin where industry standards end. And our exclusive supplier relationships ensure Lindal quality for generations to come.

TAKING THE EXTRA STEP

Virtually all structural lumber, as well as the exterior siding supplied by Lindal is kiln-dried. It's an extra step that reduces and controls moisture content, reducing the chance for twisting and warping that often occurs with green or air-dried lumber used in most new construction. Kiln-drying also reduces the weight of the wood and increases its strength, making construction easier and freight costs lower.

MAKING THE GRADE

Most of the building materials that make it into even high-end custom homes these days don't make the grade at Lindal. From beams and framing lumber to siding and floor systems, most major structural components that go into a Lindal home exceed industry standards.

PLANTING FOR THE FUTURE

Lindal supports efforts to keep forest products a sustainable resource for future generations of homeowners. Each year, through donations to tree-planting efforts and other conservation organizations, our reforestation program funds the planting of thousands of new trees — more than enough to replace the wood used in our homes.

OPPOSITE The difference in Lindal's building materials is so exceptional that even customers who hire architects to design their homes choose Lindal for quality they can't find anywhere else. Custom residence, Ontario. Customized Muskoka.

The Company

"FROM START TO FINISH, WE WERE ON BUDGET, ON TIME, AND COMPLETELY HAPPY WITH OUR LINDAL HOME AND THE LINDAL PEOPLE. WE WOULD NOT RECOMMEND BUILDING ANYTHING BUT A LINDAL."

— *Jim & Brooke Anderson, Illinois*

At the heart of the Lindal difference you'll find a history, a philosophy and a promise that have served our customers well for more than 55 years — and make our homes what they are today. Our history gives you the benefits of our knowledge, experience and teamwork as the world's leading maker of custom cedar homes. Our philosophy is based on our belief that the human spirit thrives in highly personal living environments that reflect the passions and priorities of their owners. And our promise is, quite simply, the best guarantee in the industry. Keeping that promise is the secret of our success — and your satisfaction.

A HISTORY OF BUILDING DREAMS

Lindal Cedar Homes was founded in 1945 on one man's vision to help meet the demand for new homes following World War II. Sir Walter Lindal is the founder of the company and the visionary behind its longstanding reputation for excellence. Over the years, he and his four children have remained actively involved in the management of Lindal, a publicly held company since 1971.

BRINGING OUR ADVANTAGES HOME

As the world's largest manufacturer of custom cedar homes, Lindal's size and financial strength allow us to pass volume discounts on to our customers, control quality from forest to building site, and develop new products that make your Lindal a growing pleasure to live in.

AN ENDURING COMMITMENT

A lot of things have changed since Lindal was founded. What hasn't changed is our passion for quality; we've found it never goes out of style. Neither does originality, or the art of helping people create their own vision of home. Perhaps it's our Scandinavian roots; we believe strong homes make strong communities.

HERE TODAY, HERE TOMORROW

At Lindal, we've been working closely with homeowners and evolving our company to anticipate their needs for more than half a century, continually refining and improving our ability to deliver on their dreams. The results are custom cedar homes that stand the test of time — from a company that does, too.

A GUARANTEE FOR LIFE

We're so confident of every Lindal home's lasting quality that we guarantee it. The time-proven performance of Lindal engineering and materials is the foundation of the best guarantee in the industry: a Lifetime Structural Warranty on every Lindal home. When you're making one of life's biggest investments, that's good to know.

THIS PAGE Sir Walter Lindal is Chairman Emeritus and the founder of Lindal Cedar Homes. **OPPOSITE:** 1. Meet the people behind the scenes at Lindal's corporate office in Seattle — the professionals who work closely with your local independent Lindal dealer to bring your new home to life. 2. The service and support of your Lindal dealer make a difference throughout every step of the planning process, and in your long-term satisfaction with your home. Lindal homeowners appreciate that they can be involved in the planning process as much or as little as they like. 3. Lindal Lifetime Structural Warranty — the best in the industry.

1

Lindal
2

3
THE PROMISE OF A LIFETIME
Lifetime
warranty
Lifetime Warranty
Lindal warrants that commencing one year after the home has been completed, and passed local inspection for occupancy, it will pay for the repair of major structural defects due to design or materials provided by Lindal that occur in the lifetime of the original owner. Your local Lindal dealer will be happy to provide you with full details on warranty programs.
Lindal Cedar Homes

Lindal Stories

"AFTER 55 YEARS, I STILL FEEL GREAT PRIDE AND ENTHUSIASM IN THE FACT THAT LINDAL CEDAR HOMES IS ABLE TO BRING TOGETHER FAMILIES AND THEIR DREAM HOMES."

— Sir Walter Lindal, founder Lindal Cedar Homes

LORIMER RESIDENCE, CA. COASTAL CONTEMPORARY PLAN

Every Lindal home tells a story — as unique as the people who inspired it. Join us on an armchair tour of six Lindal homes, each a deeply personal statement of the lives and styles of the people who own them. For all the diversity of their lives, locations and aesthetic tastes, they treasure their Lindal homes for many of the same reasons: fine building materials that are a world apart from other "custom" homes. Open, airy designs that allow remarkable planning flexibility. And the attention of their local Lindal dealer from start to finish. Come in and take a look around.

01

CALIFORNIA CRAFTSMAN | *Bob & Sally Young, Los Osos, California*

A soaring, two-story prow of windows looks out to a meadow lush with native oaks, grasses and wild flowers. In the distance, a backdrop of hills turns indigo in the sunset's changing light. The scent of eucalyptus, sage and lavender lingers in the warm, soft air — itself a gentle reminder that the California coastline is only minutes away. If time doesn't stand still in Los Osos, it at least invites you to slow down and stay awhile. Here, in the unspoiled natural setting that Bob and Sally Young discovered on a camping trip, is the Craftsman-inspired Lindal they call home.

"We are living in a home that 'feels right,' snuggles unobtrusively into its natural surroundings, and reflects the values of environmental respect that are so strong in this part of California."

On an acre of land just ten miles off the beaten path from San Luis Obispo, the Youngs have created a personal retreat that's at home with its natural surroundings and expresses their active lifestyle. Both Bob and Sally spend much of their working days here — he as a freelance artist, illustrator and writer; she as a retired librarian who loves children's literature and teaches graduate courses in library science.

"We wanted a house that would take advantage of the views, let in lots of light, give us the workspaces we need, and make it easy to do the kind of spontaneous entertaining we enjoy," Sally said. Although they were happy to leave behind the stresses of the Los Angeles area, they looked forward to bringing touches of their old Pasadena bungalow's Craftsman style into their new home.

Even before they bought the land, the Youngs were attracted to the open, airy designs of Lindal's post and beam building system and the warm beauty of its top grade cedar. The site confirmed their inclination: a Classic Lindal prow design seemed the perfect way to frame their view of Hollister Peak, which Bob describes as "a hill trying to be a mountain."

The Youngs' Lindal dealer, Gary Myers, visited the property before they purchased it — the first of many visits to come. "Their land has beautiful views, but it's in the middle of some sand dunes not far from a noisy four-lane road. That first visit helped us assess this issue and discuss how we could address it — through siting and insulated windows — before the Youngs even bought the land."

PREVIOUS SPREAD A two-story Lindal prow opens the back of the Youngs' home to sweeping views of their meadow and the mountains beyond. OPPOSITE Outside, the main entry's architectural details and natural materials make a dramatic opening statement. Inside, the slate floor, sage-green wall and artfully displayed Navajo "Tree of Life" rug create a welcoming first impression. THIS PAGE Bob and Sally Young with their friends, Gus and Molly, in front of their Lindal home and guest house/garage.

"Our kitchen has become a popular gathering place. People notice right away that there's something very special about this house."

Once they did, the process of planning and building became a collaboration of creativity and master craftsmanship. Using their Lindal planbook as a source of inspiration, Sally explored a number of plans before sketching a personal variation of their favorite, the Lake Vista. Gary refined her rough sketches into a working plan. "He shepherded us through the early stages of getting the first working drawings," Bob said. "There was lots of back and forth, lots of talking and playing around with things. We incorporated a number of his suggestions, including the bay window in the master bedroom and the design for the studio/garage." Over time, the studio evolved into a *(continued on page 42)*

OPPOSITE Opening to the dining room and deck, the kitchen beautifully accommodates serious cooks and impromptu guests. Cherry cabinets with ebony insets help create a warm, inviting ambiance. One side of the island welcomes guests to pull up a chair; the other side has deep drawers and a handy pull-out for trash and recyclables. The Youngs achieved a light, open feeling by opting for windows in place of upper cabinets.

THIS PAGE: LEFT A bay window brings the outdoors into the dining room, where the cedar ceiling complements the Youngs' timeless furnishings. TOP RIGHT The library's built-in shelving, high ceilings and sweeping views make a dream workspace for Sally. BOTTOM RIGHT Craftsman style comes through in ways large and small — from the work-of-art stairway to the table lamp. OPPOSITE The Youngs love to read and listen to music by the massive stone fireplace in their great room; the mantel is made from the heart of a pine tree salvaged from a forest fire. Cedar-framed prow windows frame a view of the backyard meadow and Hollister Peak. Quarter-sawn 4-inch oak floor planks add an informal touch and echo the Craftsman era.

"Our builder said that this was the best cedar he had ever seen. Our two lead carpenters were as happy as Michelangelo might have been with a fine chunk of the best available marble!"

Sunset
THE NEW YORKER

OPPOSITE Bob Young at work on a new painting in his studio, which is filled with northern light and inspirational views. THIS PAGE: LEFT A partial view of the sunroom, which has become a favorite spot for plants, pets and people to congregate. TOP RIGHT The deep tub in the skylit master bath invites soaking and stargazing. Both the shower and vanity are built for two. BOTTOM RIGHT In the master bedroom, the Youngs traded one segment of their customized bay window for a door that allows easy access to the back deck. The Lindal cedar ceiling adds warmth; astral windows add light.

(continued from page 36) charming guest house; a second outbuilding is home to Bob's art studio, which, in his words, "started out as a shed and turned into a temple."

In a happy case of serendipity, the Youngs chose a builder who works closely with an interior designer (his wife) and an architect. A native plant expert at a local nursery referred them to the landscape architect, who transformed their sandy property into a natural meadow of year-round interest and beauty. "The Youngs took an eclectic design approach, using their favorite ideas from a whole team of people," Gary said. "Clients who want to work this way are delighted to find that Lindal accommodates the process beautifully."

As construction got under way, the quality of Lindal's building materials was an inspiration to the building crew, Sally said. "The carpenters loved building this house; they were really invested in making it the most beautiful expression of their craft."

The Youngs were so delighted with the results that they brought to life a dream of Sally's, they invited the crew to sign their home — like the work of art it is. Their signatures appear on the back of the stairway next to a plaque that expresses the Youngs' appreciation: "Their care, craft and friendship are seen and felt throughout."

The living proof of the team's skill and attention to detail is visible from the moment you walk through the Youngs' front entry with its Craftsman-style posts of Colorado moss rock. By bringing together an inspired designer/builder team with Lindal's quality cedar and plans, the Youngs not only got the look of a custom Craftsman home, they got the fine materials and structural integrity that underlie the deep, abiding beauty of this style.

LINDAL CONSULTATION: *Santa Barbara Cedar Homes*

ARCHITECT: *Ernest Kim*

BUILDER: *Michael Boyack*

INTERIOR DESIGN: *Karen Boyack*

LANDSCAPE ARCHITECT: *Michael Barry*

THIS PAGE: LEFT Strength and beauty: "Both our builder and our architect were impressed by how structurally sound our home is — like Noah's ark," said Bob Young. **RIGHT** The architecture and building materials of the guest house and garage reflect the character of the main house. **OPPOSITE** With a home and a view like this, it's hard to beat your own backyard.

WINDOWS Choose windows that insulate you not only from harsh weather and climatic extremes, but from outside noise, too. Together with the quality construction of Lindal walls, Bob Young credits the double-pane low E argon windows for insulating their home from excessive road noise. "There's no question that an ordinary house would not protect us from the constant rumble."

SITE Ask your Lindal dealer to visit your site as early as possible in your planning process. Gary Myers' early visits to the Youngs' property helped them address the issue of siting before their home was designed. Going into a site with your eyes open is the key to enhancing its possibilities and avoiding any surprises later on.

PAINT Discover how much wall color can do to add warmth and character to your home. Lindal cedar looks beautiful with a wide palette of colors; don't limit yourself to white. "We were unsure of using other colors," Sally said, "but once we saw them on the walls against an unpainted section of white, we thought the white looked as cold as an iceberg."

CEDAR For added warmth and beauty anywhere in the house, line your ceilings with quality Western red cedar. It adds a dimension of richness and "finish" to a room.

THEME Consider a theme to give your home stylistic continuity. The Youngs' interior designer called their theme "casual elegance with a Craftsman touch." It was carried throughout the house in a variety of details: light fixtures, fine cherry cabinets, wide-plank oak floors and beveled-glass cabinet doors.

ARCHITECTS If you plan to consult an architect or interior designer, do so as early as possible. Find someone you feel in sync and comfortable with; after all, it's your home.

START *Month 1*
Found site and contacted Lindal dealer

PREPARATION *Month 2*
Plans developed by homeowner, Lindal, and architect

Month 7–8
Well dug, permits obtained, delivery of materials

BUILDING *Month 9–10*
Temporary power, excavation, foundation, floor system

PLANNING A CUSTOM CRAFTSMAN The Youngs chose Lindal's LakeVista plan, ℗ 89, for its prow living room, lofty second floor and sitting/office area just off the kitchen, where "Bob can work at his computer and still be in the middle of things." Here's how they personalized their plan: They flip-flopped the kitchen/dining/sitting wing to the opposite side of the living room. In its place is the master suite, which they moved from the second floor to create a private wing that mirrors the public areas at the other end of the house. Upstairs, the loft is devoted to Sally's workspace, lined with shelves of children's books and the storybook character dolls she uses in her volunteer storytelling. Just off the kitchen, the Youngs added a sunroom, a light-flooded oasis where their two dogs sleep and Sally's plants thrive. **BEDROOMS** two + office **BATHROOMS** two + three-quarter **TOTAL AREA** 2,696 sq ft **SIZE** 83' x 41'

LAKEVISTA *First floor, before plan*

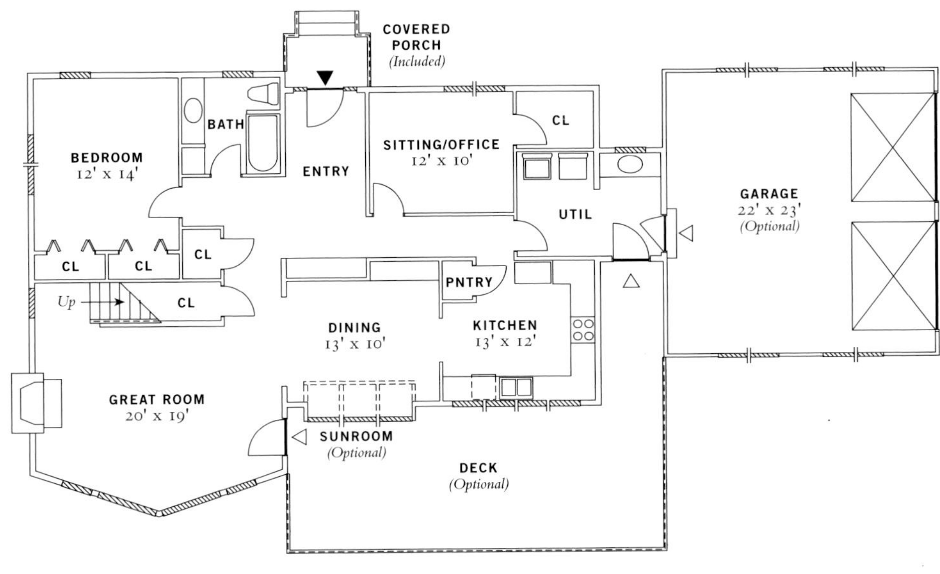

LAKEVISTA *Second floor, before plan*

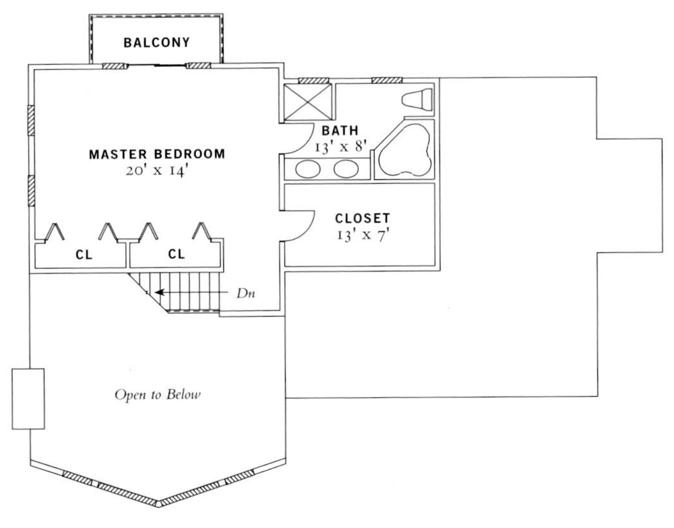

THE YOUNGS' CALIFORNIA CRAFTSMAN *First floor*

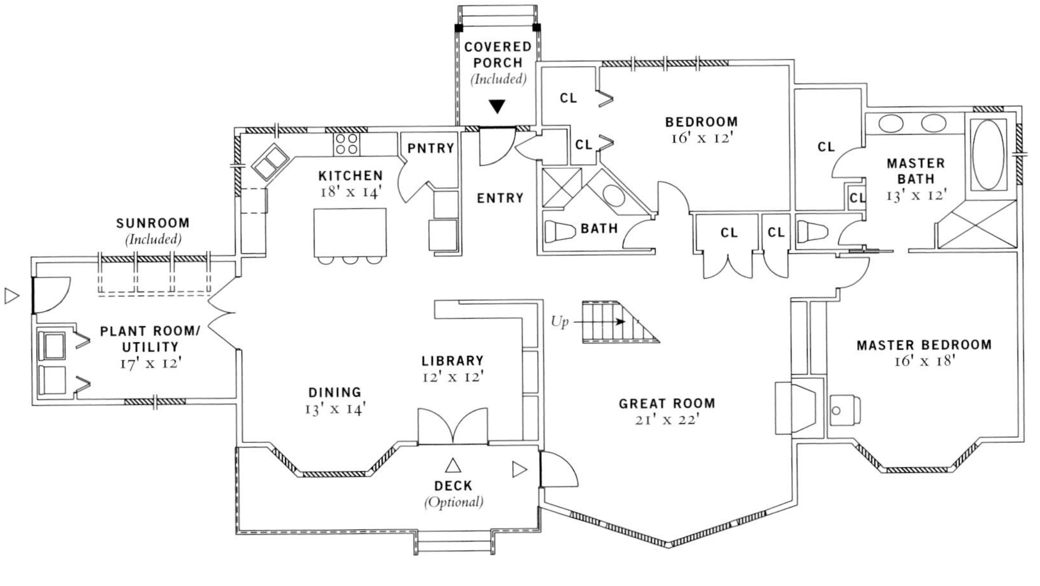

THE YOUNGS' CALIFORNIA CRAFTSMAN *Second floor*

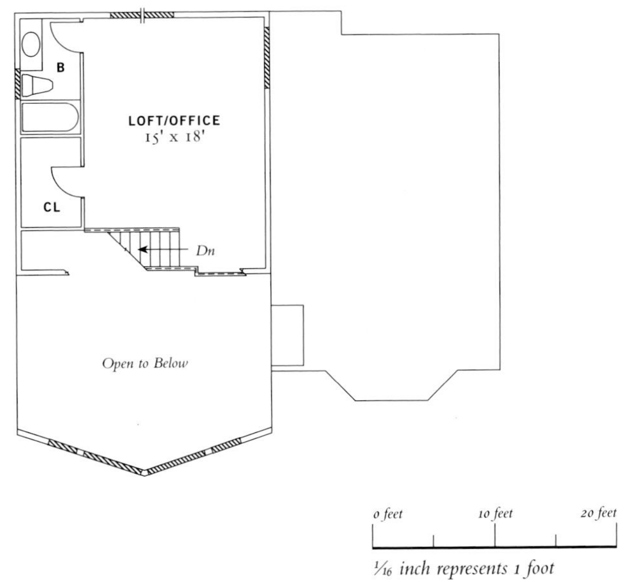

0 feet *10 feet* *20 feet*

1⁄16 inch represents 1 foot

Month 11–12
Beams, rafters, roof, windows, siding, doors, electrical

Month 13–15
Cabinets, floor covering, drywall, liner, painting

FINISH *Month 17*
Move in

Month 18
Guest house and studio

Month 21
Landscaping completed

02

NORTHWEST CHALET | *Brad & Sarah Eli, Colton, Oregon*

Nestled into a pastoral setting that has been in their family for generations, Brad and Sarah Eli's customized Lindal combines the romance of a Swiss chalet with the personal style of a most resourceful couple. To look at it, you'd never guess that such a beautifully crafted home was built on a shoestring. When the couple began planning their home, they did not have a big budget. But they did have Brad's professional carpentry skills, their initiative — and the help of family, friends and their local Lindal dealer. The bottom line? A lot of "first home" for their money.

Dr Pepper

"Lindal's kiln-dried cedar, post and beam construction, easy-to-read plans and numbered materials made it easy to build our home. So did our Lindal dealer."

From the beginning, Brad and Sarah Eli's Lindal home in Colton, Oregon, was more than a house; it was a labor of love and a win-win family arrangement. In purchasing a piece of the former cattle ranch owned by Brad's grandmother, the couple were able to build their first home close to hers. It was a nice trade-off for everyone involved, Brad said. "We are better able to take care of my grandmother here, and she gave us a good deal on the land."

Their home is inspired by one of Lindal's Classic Chalet plans. Sarah, who teaches fourth grade at the local elementary school, was immediately attracted to the Swiss architectural style of the design. From a practical point of view, Brad liked the steep pitch of the roof, which prevents rain and snow from gathering on the shingles. The size of the home was also right, he said.

"We picked the largest home we could afford — 1,371 square feet. And we added the prow front, which makes the house seem bigger."

While the Elis chose many of Lindal's cost-saving options, their home has all the strengths for which Lindals are legendary: post and beam construction, open design and peerless cedar clapboard siding. Elsewhere, Lindal's careful choice of economical, state-of-the-art products and materials lowers costs without compromising quality or style.

More savings came in the couple's willingness to be their own contractors and build most of the home themselves. As such, they especially valued the information and expertise that their Lindal dealer, Steve Conley, brought to the project.

"Steve really knew what he was talking about," Brad said. "Sarah and I would sit down with Steve and his wife, Wendy, for a few hours at a time and plan the house. Steve was right there with us when we went through the permit process with the county. Everything was on a schedule, and he met it — including getting the materials delivered on time."

"Brad and Sarah had a good idea of what they wanted in their *(continued on page 53)*

PREVIOUS SPREAD Small in scale, big on style: the main entrance to the Elis' home, which reflects the steep-roofed Swiss chalet design Sarah loves. THIS PAGE: LEFT A blooming landscape and Brad's whimsical outbuildings enhance the charm and value of this lovingly crafted home. RIGHT Sarah, Brad and Max. OPPOSITE Inside, the open floorplan unites kitchen, dining and living areas into one generous space. Cathedral ceilings make it seem even larger.

RANCHO
MIRAMAR VIJHO
NATURAL GARDEN

ANCHO
AR VIJHO
BRAND
DRINK
Pepsi-Cola
SENOR ELI
BAR & GRILL
MAZATLAN

OPPOSITE The ceiling liner and staircase of Lindal cedar add warmth and aesthetic interest to the open, airy design of the main floor. **THIS PAGE: LEFT** Crafted of knotty pine and finished with a white stain, the kitchen cabinets showcase Brad's professional cabinetmaking skills. **TOP RIGHT** The ceiling and staircase emphasize the dramatic pitch of the roof and highlight the entrance to the master suite. **BOTTOM RIGHT** Sweat equity allowed the Elis to upgrade their interior finishes, including the Mexican tiles in this bathroom.

"Lindal cedar is kiln-dried, which makes it lightweight and easy to carry. It's a huge difference from using wet wood, which is heavy and often warps."

"Our home is very energy-efficient. You can stand right by our big Lindal prow windows in the winter and not feel any cold coming through."

(continued from page 48) home," Steve said. "Based on their design criteria and budget, I sketched out a floorplan of their favorite Lindal design and gave it more of a formal entry with a true mudroom that provides an efficient traffic flow into the kitchen. We also added a walking porch with an overhang to give protection from the elements. Sometimes people want to put too many rooms into a smaller home. Brad and Sarah were smart in realizing that having fewer rooms and making them larger and more open would make their home more livable. And their original floorplan isn't overwhelmed by their new addition."

As a professional cabinetmaker with his own company, Brad was experienced enough to take on the bulk of the construction — and knowledgeable enough to hire professionals where it mattered most: for the concrete, electrical and plumbing work. The couple did the rest of the work themselves with the help of friends and family. For six months, Brad said, building their home was their life. "There were a lot of late nights during that time. Sometimes I'd stay until midnight."

Lindal made his job easier every step of the way, Brad said. "The plans are easy to read. And Lindal's materials are great to build with. The cedar is kiln-dried, so it's lighter weight and easier to carry. Plus our wood never warped; our sheetrock has never cracked because all the Lindal wood was dry. That's a huge difference from the weight and warping problems you have with wet wood. Plus every Lindal board comes numbered, which is really nice. And any time I had a question, I'd call Steve and he'd have the answer."

Three years after Brad and Sarah finished their home, they welcomed their first child, Max Enzo, into the world. With this new addition to the family, the couple has expanded the main floor of their home. Now one side

door opens into a 632-square-foot addition with a bedroom, an office and a family/billiard room complete with wet bar.

For the Elis, the joys of building their own home were deepened by the fact that their friends and family had a hand in it. "Because we built our home ourselves, I think we feel more comfortable in it," Brad said. "So do our friends and family. They feel like it's their home, too."

LINDAL CONSULTATION: *CedarCraft Northwest*

BUILDER: *The Elis, friends and family*

INTERIOR DESIGN: *The Elis*

OPPOSITE The great room's prow windows look out to a secluded field enclosed by evergreens. The Elis chose Lindal vinyl-framed windows for economy and energy efficiency. **THIS PAGE: LEFT** A labor of love in process: the addition to the Elis' home was designed with the help of Lindal, built with the help of friends and family. **RIGHT** Brad crafted these birdhouses from leftover cedar.

SWEAT EQUITY Keep total labor costs to a minimum by exchanging "sweat equity" with people you know. It's the way a lot of homes used to be built. Not only is it economical, it's a good feeling to live in a house built with the love and labor of friends and family.

COST CUTTING Doing some of the finish work yourself saves money that can go toward building a larger home or upgrading your finish materials. It also gives you personal pride in a job well done. The Elis splurged on Mexican ceramic tile for their bathroom floor, but Sarah and her mother totally eliminated labor costs by laying the tile themselves.

CONTRACT WORK Do not, however, skimp on professional know-how when it comes to plumbing, electrical and concrete work, the Elis advise. Mistakes can be too expensive and even hazardous to leave these jobs to well-intentioned do-it-yourselfers.

SPACE If you're planning a relatively small home, the Elis suggest flowing together the living, kitchen and eating areas into one great room. The Lindal prow and cathedral ceilings further enhance the sense of spaciousness in their home.

TIGHT BUDGETS Focus on your priorities to make the most of a tight budget. For example, adding the prow to the great room and putting a balcony off the master bathroom were important to the Elis. But matching the colors of their bathroom fixtures was not; they saved lots of money on factory seconds in slightly different shades.

EXPANDING Take any plans for future expansion into account as you design your home. Knowing what and where you'll add on can save you time and money, make the addition easier to do — and result in a larger home that works well and looks "in scale."

START *Month 1*
Found site and contacted Lindal dealer

PREPARATION *Month 3–6*
Building site analysis, plans developed by homeowner and Lindal, arrange financing

Month 7
Temporary power, excavation, foundation, subcontractors

NORTHWEST CHALET When Brad and Sarah Eli began planning their Lindal home, they expected to add on to it someday. So they planned their original home with an easy expansion in mind. Three years later, after their first child was born, they revisited Lindal dealer Steve Conley to design a 632-square-foot addition to the main floor. As before, Brad used Lindal's kiln-dried cedar and easy-to-follow plans to build the addition himself with the help of friends and family. This new wing, located on one side of the prow, adds a bedroom, a home office and a billiard room to the Elis' home, more than doubling their living space. **BEDROOMS** three + office **BATHROOMS** one + three-quarter **TOTAL AREA: BEFORE REMODEL** 1,371 sq ft **AFTER REMODEL** 2,003 sq ft **SIZE** 48' x 41'

NORTHWEST CHALET
First floor, before remodel

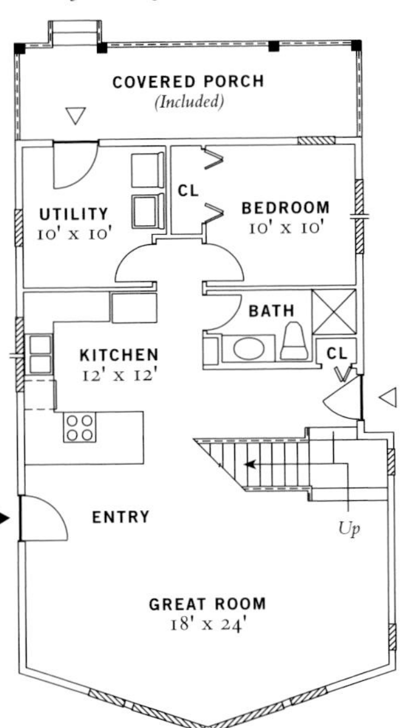

NORTHWEST CHALET
Second floor, before remodel

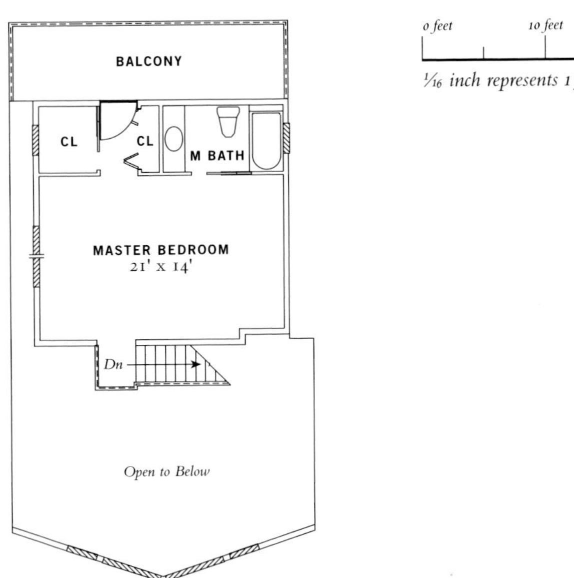

0 feet *10 feet* *20 feet*

1/16 inch represents 1 foot

ELIS' CUSTOM CHALET
First floor, after remodel

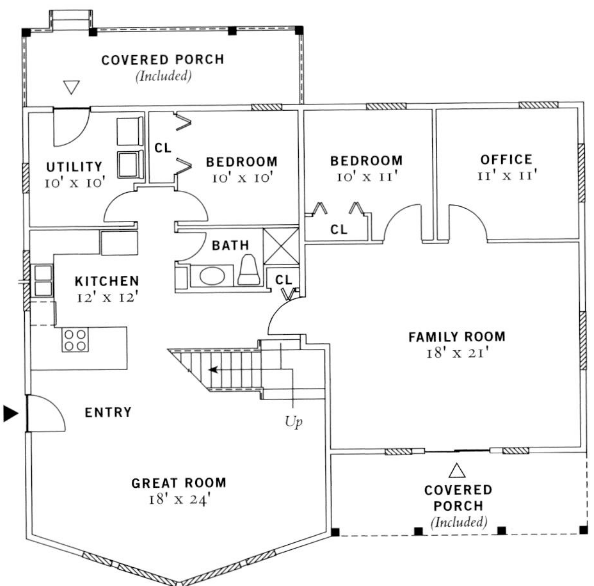

ELIS' CUSTOM CHALET
Second floor, after remodel

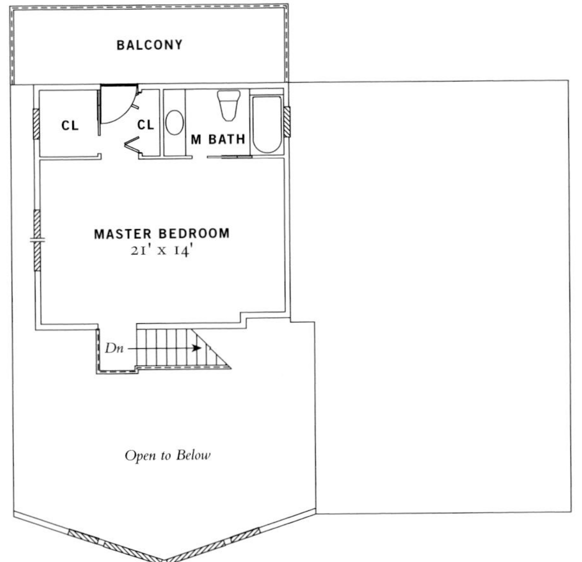

Month 8
Delivery of materials, subcontractors

BUILDING *Month 9*
Beams, rafters, roof, windows, siding, doors

Month 10–11
Drywall, liner, painting, cabinets, floor covering

Month 12
Move in, landscaping, driveways, grass

03

COASTAL CONTEMPORARY | *Rod & Sally Lorimer, Albion, California*

There aren't many opportunities in life to trade urban living for a rural setting — exchanging crowds and clutter for for clean space and the warmth of a smaller community. For Rod and Sally Lorimer, the creation of their custom Lindal home was just such a chance. They distilled their dream to a few deep desires: a high ridge top overlooking the rugged Mendocino coastline, crowned with a passive-solar Lindal so open to the natural wonders around it that the Pacific light and awe-inspiring views are an integral part of their home. With a custom Lindal as spectacular as all outdoors, who could ask for more?

Like a haiku verse that says it all in a few well-chosen words, the Lorimers' original Lindal home edits out the extraneous to let the essential shine through. Here the major inspirations come from nature: the lavish light that bathes the rooms in a radiant glow, the grace of a hawk gliding against a backdrop of sea and sky, the briny scent of an ocean breeze, the sounds of surf and sea life 400 feet below.

Having lived in many homes over the course of Rod's corporate career, the Lorimers approached this one with a clear notion of what is important to them: Lots of light. Lots of glass looking out to uninterrupted scenic views. The enduring beauty and low maintenance of cedar. An open, flowing floorplan that only post and beam construction makes possible. All of these priorities led them to Lindal.

PREVIOUS SPREAD Protected from ocean winds, an Asian-inspired garden flourishes in the courtyard of the Lorimers' sleek contemporary home. Lindal vertical cedar siding is a natural in the coastal setting. **THIS PAGE: ABOVE** Sally and Rod Lorimer with their yellow Labrador, Nikki. **OPPOSITE** On the ocean side, Lindal engineering supports double walls of two-story windows that seem to reach for the sky.

"People tell us that every window looks like it's framing a painting of the ocean, the valley, the trees or the little red barn — the only other building in sight."

"We've always wanted a cedar home," Rod said. "After comparing alternatives, we found Lindal Cedar Homes offered the best value for the highest quality."

The strengths of Lindal's classic post and beam building system allowed the glass-intensive home to be situated right where the couple wanted it on their 20 acres of high coastal meadow. Perched on a knoll above the confluence of Salmon Creek and the Pacific Ocean, the prominent site affords spectacular 270-degree views — and exposes the home to high winds and winter storms.

"Lindal's engineering allowed our architect to design huge, open expanses without support posts — and meet California's tough coastal building codes to withstand high winds," Rod said. "During the winter, we often experience rainstorms with winds of 50 to 80 miles per hour. Our home takes them without a whimper or a leak."

Their home also weathers cold spells with low heating costs, thanks to a passive-solar design that provides nearly half of the home's heat. The sun's heat is gathered and stored in the ceramic-tile floors and circulated through water coils. Careful site planning and design maximize the energy efficiency of the passive-solar design. In summer, when the sun is high, the home is designed to block its rays from entering and overheating the interior. In winter, when the sun is lower, it becomes a welcome source of warmth and light.

Throughout the home, the floorplan and furnishings reflect the couple's passion for clean lines and uncluttered spaces. The entire main floor is a graceful flow of space unified by a breathtaking focal point: a wall of windows and two sets of sliding doors opening onto the ocean-view deck. Filled with light and coastal panoramas, the spacious sweep of the dining room, kitchen, great room and adjacent "Sunset Room" create an easy, relaxed ambiance that welcomes everything from intimate family gatherings to neighborhood potlucks of 30 or more. At either end of the U-shaped home, the master suite and guest *(continued on page 65)*

THIS PAGE: LEFT The fireplace is surrounded by a two-story wall of windows that flood the living room with natural light and panoramas. **RIGHT** From the loft, Rod has a top-of-the-world ocean view. **OPPOSITE** Lindal engineering allows an open flow of space, which is visually reinforced by the room-to-room continuity of ceramic floor tiles and the elimination of upper kitchen cabinets.

OPPOSITE With its open design, elegant materials and art at every turn, the kitchen is an inviting place to entertain; "his-and-her" sinks make it easy for two cooks to collaborate. **TOP RIGHT** The kitchen's granite-top island has room to accommodate eating and food preparation. **BOTTOM RIGHT** Even the cedar-ceilinged guest bath has a double-sink vanity and a spectacular view.

"We wanted our home to be wonderful, but low maintenance. That led us to Lindal."

(continued from page 60) bedroom have the meditative calm of the Asian-inspired garden courtyard they surround.

True to the spirit of Japanese style interpreted so sensitively in the home's interior design and details, everything is either useful or beautiful — or both. Ample built-in storage eliminates the need for bedroom dressers or upper kitchen cabinets that would impose on a wonderful view. In many places, what's not included is as telling as what is. Why build a traditional mantle when the fireplace can be surrounded by a wall of glass looking out to the ocean? Why hem in the spacious luxury of a shower for two when eliminating the door altogether transforms it into an open, spa-like environment? This is a home where original thinking has triumphed over the conventional to create a truly personal living environment. By asking themselves all the right questions early on in the planning process, the Lorimers came up with answers that work beautifully for the way they want to live.

LINDAL CONSULTATION: *Cedar Homes by Bonari*
ARCHITECT: *Leventhal and Schlosser*
INTERIOR DESIGN CONSULTANT: *Ricia Araiza*
LANDSCAPE DESIGN: *The Lorimers*

OPPOSITE Beyond the light-bathed Sunset Room, the master bedroom is a sanctuary of serenity and Asian style — with easy access to the oceanside deck and hot tub. **THIS PAGE: TOP** Mirrors above the double-sink vanity multiply the light and views in the master bath. **BOTTOM** A skylight illuminates the two-person shower.

BEDROOMS Let your lifestyle be your guide to the location of your home's bedrooms. While family bedrooms are often clustered together, the Lorimers created a gracious sense of privacy for their guest bedroom by placing it at the opposite end of the house from the master bedroom.

PASSIVE SOLAR The right siting is crucial to passive solar-design, which relies on carefully planned angles of sunlight for success. Knowing that even a few degrees can make a big difference, the Lorimers visited their building site many times to track the path of sunlight across a particular tree — especially where it fell at daybreak and sunset.

CEDAR Want to enjoy the beauty of Lindal cedar ceilings while toning down the contrast to surrounding drywall? It's easy to do. The Lorimers' cedar ceilings were painted with the same color as their drywall — then wiped to let the grain of the wood show through. The effect: a polished, all-of-a-tone tranquillity.

STORAGE Plan plenty of storage and workspace into the kitchen. The Lorimers' "his-and-her" sinks and uninterrupted lengths of countertop make it a pleasure to prepare a meal together. Roomy roll-out drawers and a walk-in pantry provide ample storage without upper cabinets obstructing their views.

SIDING For a beachy-looking, low-maintenance exterior, the Lorimers applied a bleaching oil to their Lindal cedar siding. The oil hastens the cedar's transformation to that natural silver-gray color that's so at home by the ocean; one or two applications eliminate the need for periodic staining or painting.

PLANNING AHEAD Prioritize and plan for the things that will make the greatest difference to you in the daily enjoyment of your home. For the Lorimers, light — natural and otherwise — was at the top of the list. "Early on, we spent a lot of time designing the lighting into the home," Sally Lorimer said.

START *Month 1–3*
Found site and contacted Lindal dealer

PREPARATION *Month 7–8*
Plans developed by homeowner, Lindal, and architect

Month 9–10
Permits obtained

Month 11–12
Contacted builder and subcontractors

Month 15
Delivery of materials

PLANNING A COASTAL CONTEMPORARY Inspired by Lindal's classic post and beam construction, the Lorimers wanted a contemporary, clean lined home that visually let in the outdoors. Lindal's structural integrity gave them the design flexibility to make the most of their ocean bluff site and desire for passive solar energy. Their Lindal dealer worked closely with their architect's design to create an engineered system that supports the wide, open spaces and windows they love. "Our Lindal dealer, Leo Bonari, was an advocate for us," Rod Lorimer said. "As we worked with the architect and the builder, he represented our views and straightened out any loose ends."

"We cherry-picked the things we've liked best about all of the houses we've lived in," Sally said. The home's U-shaped footprint wraps 3,300 square feet of living space around a large central courtyard, where a flourishing garden is protected from high winds. Above the kitchen area, a loft takes the dramatic views to another level. Furnished with easy chairs, books and a computer workspace, it looks out to sweeping vistas in three directions. All major main-floor living spaces have sliding glass doors that open to ocean breezes and expansive decking with a perfectly situated hot tub. **BEDROOMS** two + office **BATHROOMS** one + three-quarter **TOTAL AREA** 3,300 sq ft **SIZE** 87' x 78'

COASTAL CONTEMPORARY
First floor

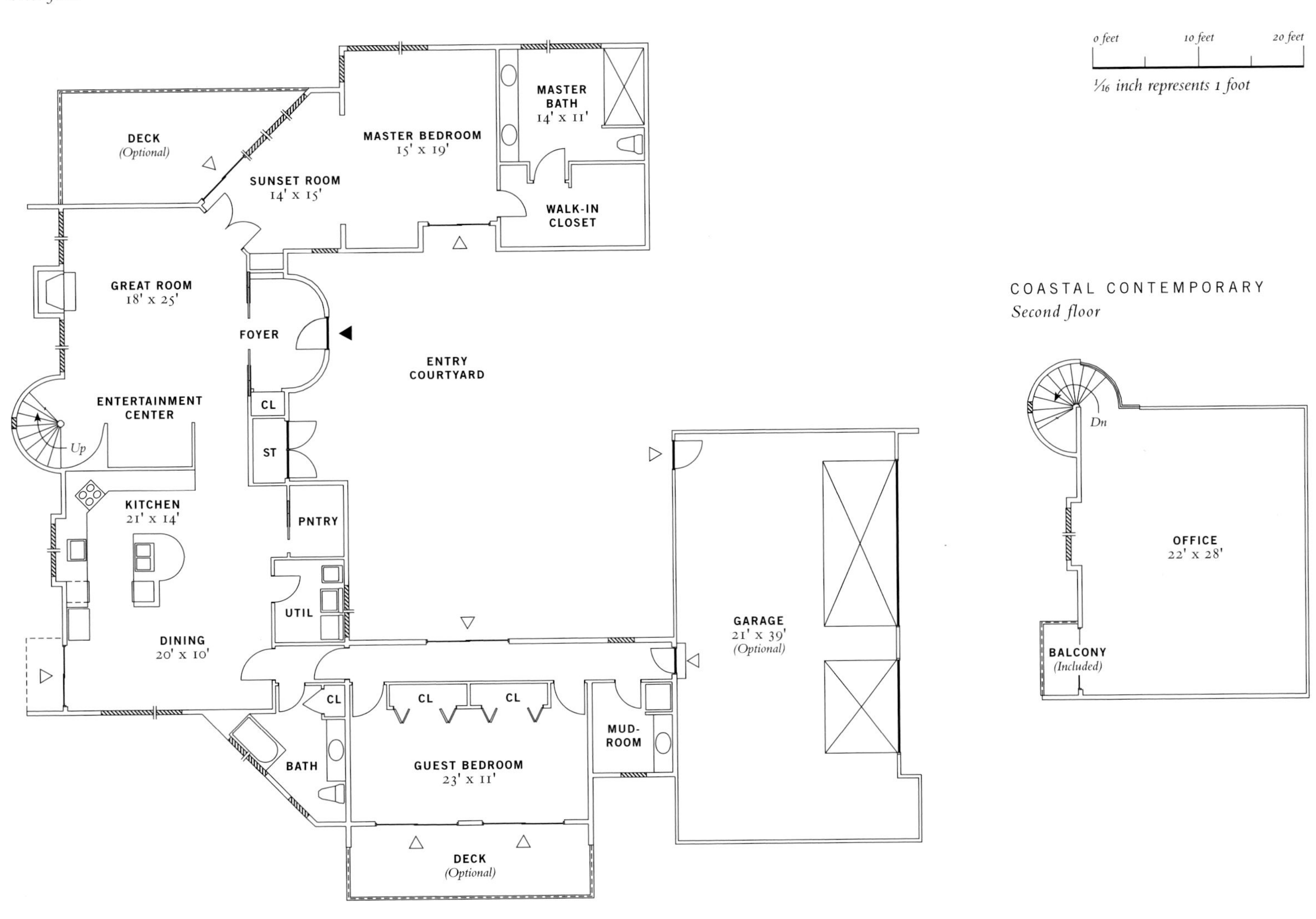

BUILDING *Month 16*
Temporary power, excavation, foundation, floor system

Month 17–19
Beams, rafters, roof, windows, siding, doors

Month 20–21
Plumbing, electrical, insulation, drywall, liner, painting

Month 23
Cabinets, floor coverings

FINISH *Month 28*
Move in, ongoing landscaping

04

RIDGETOP RANCH | *Colleen & Larry Kling, Eagle, Idaho*

When Colleen and Larry Kling decided to return to their roots and their passion for ranching, they knew that no ordinary "mini-ranch" would do. Neither would an ordinary home. On 185 acres of ranch land crowning High Ridge Lane in Eagle, Idaho, the Klings built the ultimate log home, a custom Lindal crafted of solid cedar timbers. This living wonder of finely finished cedar and Lindal engineering has been their dream ever since Colleen ran her hand down a velvet-smooth railing at a Lindal model home many years ago and said to herself, "Someday I have to have one of these."

Surrounded in every direction by wide-open ranch land, the Klings' solid cedar Lindal reflects the appeal of its ridge top setting — an exhilarating sense of spaciousness, glorious light and 360-degree views. With corporate life and a successful trucking business behind them, the couple have created a home that helped them open a new chapter in their lives. Now their days are devoted to their love of ranching, horseback riding and team penning, the sport of separating three cattle from a herd of 30.

Outdoors, the couple's life revolves around their 14 quarter horses and more than 300 head of cattle. Indoors, their home is filled with the easy ambiance

PREVIOUS SPREAD Visitors who follow the rustic split-wood fence to the Klings' ranch find a solid cedar Lindal sited and designed to capture breathtaking views in every direction. THIS PAGE: ABOVE Colleen and Larry Kling take a break from working with their horses. OPPOSITE Lindal design, engineering and the fine finish of Lindal solid cedar timbers bring a whole new level of comfort and style to log home living.

"Our solid cedar home is cool in the summer and warm in the winter. We've never felt a draft. Everyone who comes into this house remarks on the warmth of the wood. And maintenance is a piece of cake."

and mementos of ranch living. Trophy saddles, spurs, antique chaps, horse blankets, Navajo and antique rugs are at home with the solid cedar timbers that form the walls of their Lindal.

"Larry and Colleen wanted an open, airy look that was rustic but elegant," said the Klings' Lindal dealers. "We called it 'nouveau cowboy.' We worked with them to come up with a plan that suited their lifestyle and their property."

Having lived in 11 homes over the course of their corporate life, the couple knew they wanted to go beyond the conventional structure this time around. "We wanted a home that had character — one we could really live in," Colleen said. "In some of our other homes, we rarely went into the living room. Here, we wear our boots in it."

They compared log homes from a number of companies before choosing Lindal's optional solid cedar wall construction. "Lindal allowed us to do a real custom home," Colleen said.

Lindal's 4-by-8-inch solid cedar timbers brought to life the rugged practicality and light-filled elegance they envisioned. "The wood is so durable, yet it has the feeling of fine furniture," Colleen said. "We also liked the openness of Lindal's classic post and beam building system. It allows such a spacious feeling."

Lindal engineering made it possible to incorporate all the glass the Klings wanted — including the walls of windows in the dramatic prow that is the focal point of the home. "You might think all this space and so much glass would have a cold feeling," Colleen said. "But you get the warmth of all this wood."

The interior magic comes from the Klings' lavish use of wood and glass — an inspiring example of what happens when light is understood and incorporated as a design element. "We situated and customized the home to take advantage of the views and have sunlight come in all day long," Colleen said. True to her Scandinavian heritage, she looks forward to her early morning ritual of having a cup of good coffee and watching the day begin. "To sit in the sunroom or kitchen by the Norwegian wood-burning stove with the light streaming into the room as I have my coffee — that was really important to me."

Other personal design decisions add comfort and convenience throughout the house. "We custom-designed the rooms to suit our lifestyles,"

Colleen said. "With the kids grown, we made the bedrooms smaller and placed greater emphasis on the living areas, upstairs and down. We built a second kitchen downstairs so we could entertain there without *(continued on page 79)*

OPPOSITE: TOP The Klings' sun-filled kitchen includes a versatile island and a separate counter and sink devoted to the art of coffee making. **BOTTOM LEFT AND RIGHT** Just off the kitchen, the sunroom is the couple's favorite place to begin the day. **THIS PAGE** Surrounded by views of their ranch land, the Klings enjoy the morning light in their breakfast nook.

THIS PAGE: TOP A wide, gracious stairway leads to another full level of living space. Flanked by a wall of windows that follow the soaring roofline and overlook the ranch, the river-rock fireplace is the heart of the living room. **OPPOSITE** Light, airy and energy efficient, the Klings' solid cedar Lindal is a world apart from typical log homes. The Klings rarely used the living rooms in most of their previous homes; this one gets lived in.

OPPOSITE Lindal's solid cedar timbers create a warm, restful ambiance in the master suite, complete with a full bath with jetted tub and a commanding view of the surrounding ranchlands. THIS PAGE: LEFT The radiant glow and natural fragrance of Lindal cedar are daily pleasures in the baths of this contemporary log home. RIGHT A guest bedroom any visiting cowhand is sure to love.

"There is absolutely nothing like cedar ceilings and walls at night. When they're lit with muted light, there's a glow you just can't get from any other material."

(continued from page 73) coming upstairs." With its generous seating, remarkable views and full kitchen, the downstairs recently hosted 100 guests for their nephew's wedding. Together with the downstairs guest bedroom, bath and living area, that second kitchen creates the popular Cowboy Suite, the family's name for the private guest quarters decorated in Western motif.

Special touches in the main kitchen cater to the couple's personal tastes, including a coffee bar with its own storage space and sink. Some of the kitchen drawers have convenient pop-up countertops that add surface area as needed. The adjacent sunroom opens the entire kitchen to breathtaking mountain views — complete with a table for breakfast and a telescope for nighttime stargazing. "We almost didn't include a sunroom in our plans," Colleen said. "Then one day we were sitting in our dealer's Lindal sunroom making plans and I realized we had to have one."

Along with the splendor of the Klings' property comes the challenges of bitter-cold winters and high winds that sweep across the ridge. Lindal's Energy Lock™ walls eliminate the draftiness typical of log homes, keeping the home snug and warm in even the most severe Idaho weather. The solid cedar walls store the sun's warmth during the day and release it slowly and evenly as temperatures drop at night. Together, Lindal's energy-efficient engineering and passive-solar design keep the home comfortable, and the energy bills low, all year.

"With a solid cedar home, the wood is its own insulation," Colleen said. "It's cool in the summer and warm in the winter. Even when it's cold and windy outside, you get this wonderfully warm, cozy feeling inside. I've had so many homes with white walls, and they seem so much colder. Our heating bill is about half the price you'd expect for a home of this size."

Together, Colleen and Larry have created a warm, inviting hilltop haven that people hate to leave — guests and owners alike.

"When we travel, we wish we could lift up this home and take it with us," Colleen said. "It embodies everything we love. It's spacious and filled with light, yet it's warm and cozy because of all this wonderful wood.

"It's a lovely house to come home to."

OPPOSITE The Klings have easy access to their deck; the entire home was carefully sited and designed to capture sunlight and views from their Ridgetop Ranch. THIS PAGE: LEFT French doors lead into Larry's den just off the master suite. RIGHT Small, dark rooms and predictably boxy spaces are refreshingly absent from this log home — even on the lower level.

LINDAL CONSULTATION: *Rick & Jan Stanley*

INTERIOR DESIGN: *Debra King, Design Spectrum, Boise*

KITCHEN DESIGN: *Mary Ann's Kitchen Planning of Boise*

DECOR Don't waste space and money on rooms or decor that are more for looks than for living, says Colleen Kling. Forget the idealized images of home and invest in things that support how you want to live and what makes you happy. To wit: don't buy a white carpet if what you really want to do is stroll around the house in your cowboy boots.

CEDAR WALLS Solid cedar walls pose different decorating challenges — and opportunities — than does painted drywall. The Klings' rustic ranch decor works wonderfully with the rich beauty of their interior wood. So do lodge-like furnishings and any natural theme, from beaches and lakes to forests and mountains.

BUILT-INS Devote the same attention to built-in storage in other parts of the house that you do to your kitchen. Design around the things you own. Have drawers, shelves and other custom built-ins designed to accommodate clothes and accessories. Include storage for every television, VCR, stereo and computer in your plans.

SPECIAL CONSIDERATIONS One of the joys of a custom home is the ability to design peaceful coexistence where it matters most. In the Klings' home, special insulation between the master bedroom and bath allows an early riser to be up and around without waking the other person.

KITCHENS If your dream includes a professional-caliber kitchen, you may want to consult a kitchen planning specialist. The Klings found it helpful to work with a kitchen planner — and easy to incorporate the ideas into their Lindal design.

COLLECTIONS Showcase the things that mean a lot to you; they make a home your own. Over the years, the Klings have collected treasures that they display throughout their home, adding personality to every room and expressing their love for horses, ranching and Western life.

START *Month 1–2*
Found site and contacted Lindal dealer

PREPARATION *Month 5*
Plans developed by homeowner, and Lindal

Month 10
Financing arranged, contractors selected, permits obtained

Month 11–12
Temporary power, excavation, foundation, delivery of materials

VIEW LIVING ON EVERY LEVEL The Klings' home is inspired by Lindal's CliffSide plan, Ⓟ 74, a two-story contemporary with vaulted ceilings and a soaring prow. Together, the two levels and wings on either side of the prow multiply the opportunities for views.

On the main floor, the Klings reversed the master bedroom and kitchen wings and added two bedrooms on either side of the foyer. The kitchen wing was reconfigured to embrace a breakfast nook and sunroom in one open expanse. Larry's den was added just off the living room. Sliding doors and decking were eliminated directly off the prow in favor of a river-rock fireplace framed by the wall of windows. Spacious decks flank both sides of the prow and are accessible from the master suite, living room and kitchen areas.

The lower level includes the self-contained Cowboy Suite with a complete second kitchen. The suite opens onto the game room with its big-screen TV, desk and seating for a crowd. Having added more bedrooms upstairs, the Klings devoted one wing of the lower level to a roomy garage. **BEDROOMS** three + office **BATHROOMS** two + three-quarter **TOTAL AREA** 4,344 sq ft **SIZE** 94' x 48'

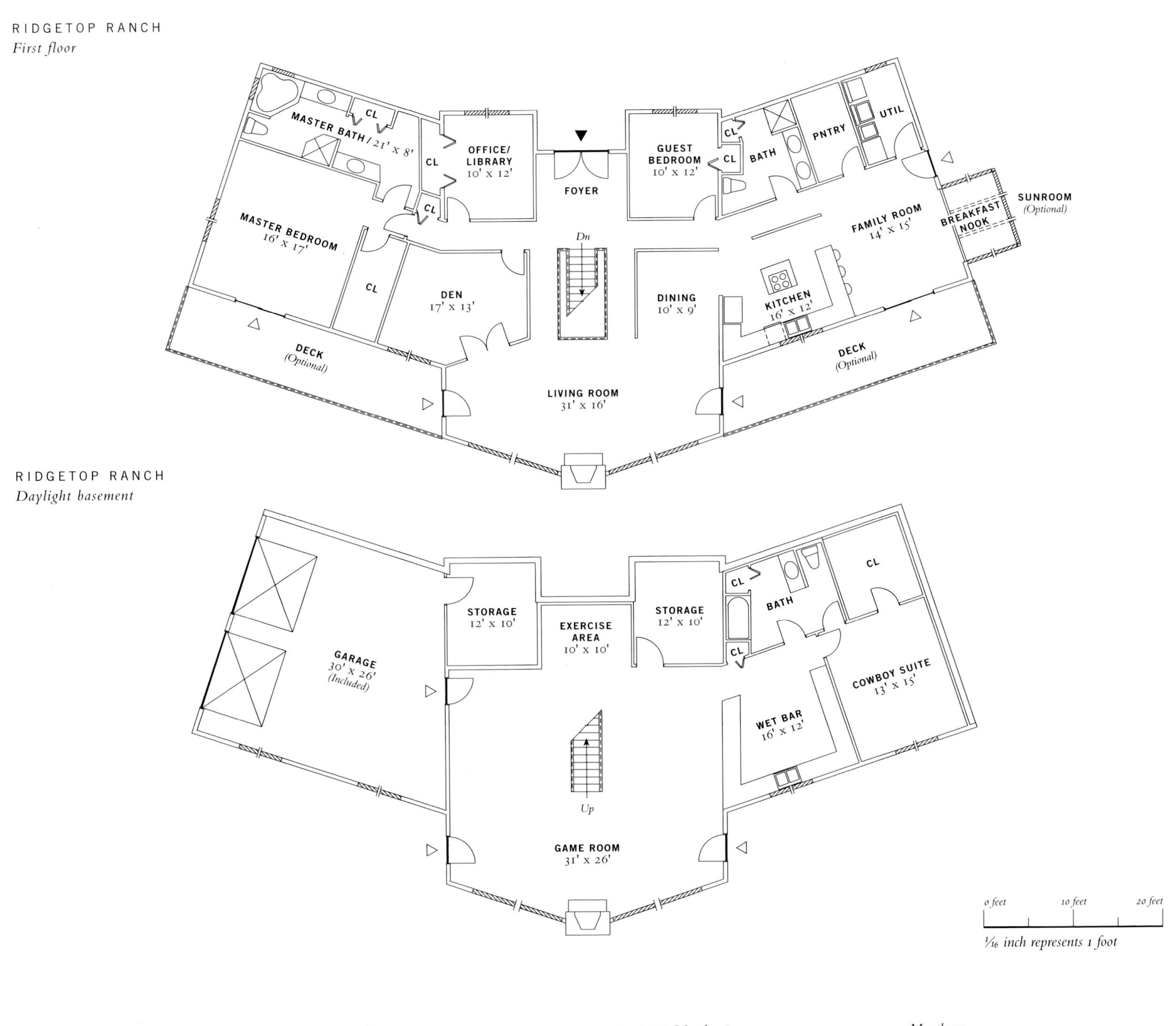

BUILDING *Month 13–15*
Floor system, beams, rafters, roof, windows, siding, doors

Month 16–17
Drywall, liner, painting, cabinets, floor covering

FINISH *Month 18–19*
Landscaping

Month 20
Move in

05

How do you design a sense of delight and discovery into a compact living space? The answers are everywhere in this 1,800-square-foot Lindal home. Created by Lindal in partnership with *Home* magazine, it reflects the charm, comfort and efficiency of Finland's traditional summer cottages. Gale Steves, editor-in-chief of the magazine; took on the homeowner's role, describing a vision inspired by her travels through Finland to Lindal dealers Jim and Susan Johnston. Gale enlisted interior designer Elizabeth Gaynor, author of *Finland Living Design*, who furnished the home in cooperation with the Finland Trade Center in New York. From the yellow front door to the back porch sauna, Lindal design and craftsmanship capture the pleasures of Finnish country homes in every square foot.

World renowned for its mastery of beautiful and useful design, the Finns' architectural vernacular instills even their smallest homes with inspirational style and livability. This Lindal home does, too. It embodies a traditional Scandinavian way of seeing and living in the domestic world that has growing universal appeal in the 21st century. Not a single square foot is wasted — functionally or aesthetically. Many spaces have multiple uses. And design attention is lavished on the sensory delights of daily living — from carefully placed windows that let in light and air, to the heart-of-the-home fireplace in the great room and the dreamy window seat tucked into one dramatic wall of the master bedroom.

"The ability to incorporate a wide world of styles and design influences is a big advantage of working with Lindal," local dealer Jim Johnston said. "In this case, we took Gale's lead; she traveled *(continued on page 89)*

PREVIOUS SPREAD This small home is big on exterior style — with gabled dormers, a full-length porch and traditional Finnish colors. THIS PAGE: ABOVE A bird's-eye view of the great room from the loft. OPPOSITE Open to the kitchen and dining room, the great room is "anchored" by an energy-efficient Tulikivi soapstone stove from Finland.

FINLAND

THIS PAGE: LEFT Cedar-framed Lindal windows and a sliding glass door bring natural light and scenes of the outdoors into the dining room. **TOP RIGHT** Strategically placed above the sink: a bottomless cupboard with built-in dish drainer. **BOTTOM RIGHT** The range is flanked by convenient counters and cabinets; the hood's elegant lines add a lyrical beauty to the room. **OPPOSITE** Massive beams are a warm, natural accent to the kitchen's cool gray countertops, white cupboards and stainless steel fixtures. The stainless steel refrigerator is matched by a stainless steel pantry at the other end of the counter.

"While compact, this 1,800-square-foot Lindal home has a feeling of light and spaciousness, thanks to the soaring rooflines typical of post and beam construction." — *Gale Steves, editor-in-chief,* Home *magazine*

(continued from page 84) all over Finland gathering the ideas and inspirations that we designed into this home."

Finnish style begins with a dwelling's sensitivity to its surrounding environment. Honoring the Finnish concept of *sointu* (harmony or balance), the home is situated on a hill in its rural setting to take full advantage of views and abundant natural light. The building site itself yielded the large boulders used in the landscaping, which is visually softened by the mass of mature trees left untouched.

Inside, interconnected main-floor living spaces echo the one-room living characteristic of Finnish log cabins, which were among the first in the world. The great room is open to the kitchen and dining room, which expands the sense of space and makes for easy, relaxed entertaining. It's a living example of *tupa* — the Finnish word for a large, open living area that comfortably accommodates a multitude of uses. Tall windows and a ceiling that reaches 16 feet at its peak enhance the spacious, airy feeling of Lindal's classic post and beam construction; a freestanding fireplace adds a focal point for gatherings of family and friends.

The more private living spaces of the master suite and home office loft are clustered into the cozy upper floor. Here the ceilings continue to follow the roofline, creating more magical spaces. In the master suite, a gabled dormer embraces a window seat — the perfect place to curl up with a good book. In the home office, a Lindal SkyWall contributes to a lofty, treehouse atmosphere.

True to Finnish tradition, storage is abundant and well planned throughout the house. The master suite includes a large walk-in closet, located just off the master bath. In the kitchen, the built-in buffet counter that borders the great room provides adjustable shelving to display books or other treasures. Perhaps the most telling example of Finnish ingenuity is the

OPPOSITE Lindal cedar lines the high ceilings of the upstairs home office. Black-and-white shades provide a graphic window treatment for the Lindal SkyWall. **THIS PAGE: LEFT** True to Finnish tradition, the Nordic sauna is easily accessible to the outdoors — just steps from an outdoor shower on the back porch. **RIGHT** The blue-and-white master bath features a double-sink vanity, a whirlpool tub and a separate custom shower.

FINLAND

“This Lindal home uses space to the maximum; every inch is lived in.”

— *Gale Steves, editor-in-chief,* Home *magazine*

bottomless cupboard above the kitchen sink; rinsed dishes can be placed directly into its built-in draining rack and allowed to drip-dry.

Just as important to Finnish style as the versatile spaces are the materials that create them. Like the Finns, Lindal has a passion for using fine wood inside and out. Outside, Lindal's Western red cedar siding is painted a classic Finnish red and accented with crisp white trim. Inside, wood-framed windows, doors and beams maintain the color of the natural material. In the home office, radiant Lindal cedar lines the high ceiling for added warmth.

No one visits this home without commenting on its playful but sophisticated use of color — a Finnish decorative tradition that Lindal building materials complement beautifully. Buttery yellows, denim blues and accents of rustic red and black are comfortable companions to crisp white and the warm tones of Lindal's fine-as-furniture Western red cedar.

In the unerring eyes of Gale Steves, who travels far and wide searching out special residences to grace the pages in *Home,* this Finnish-inspired Lindal design is a tribute to life on a smaller, simpler scale. It's part of a growing awareness that scaling down doesn't have to mean settling for less.

LINDAL CONSULTATION: *Atlantic Custom Homes*
BUILDER: *Bill Burhans, Custom Country Homes*
INTERIOR DESIGN: *Elizabeth Gaynor*

OPPOSITE A gabled dormer creates a dramatic wall and window seat in the master bedroom. **THIS PAGE: TOP** The beauty of this sunny guest room is in its crisp, comfortable efficiency: plenty of light, storage, creature comforts — and an adjacent bathroom. **BOTTOM** The children's bedroom is computer-friendly.

HARMONY Before you take out that tree or level the ground, consider the aesthetic merits and cost savings of planning your home in harmony with its natural surroundings. Mature trees are a treasure worth saving; natural elevations can enhance the character and aesthetic appeal of your site.

MULTIPLE USES To make the most of every square foot of your home, design and furnish some rooms to accommodate multiple uses. Perhaps a home office can double as an occasional guest bedroom. With a few dozen square feet, you can carve out a quiet sitting area or an exercise alcove in the master suite. A wall of built-in bookshelves can transform a living room into a comfortable library.

BEAMS Exposed Lindal beams are a stylish way to bring the strength and beauty of wood into a room. They can transform an ordinary ceiling into an extraordinary architectural statement. Imagine how different the kitchen and great room of this home would look without the visual impact of those beams.

CEILINGS AND WINDOWS High ceilings and well-placed windows add a sense of expansiveness to a small home. With its two-story ceiling, the great room in this Lindal home extends not only horizontally, into the dining room and kitchen, but vertically — toward the sky.

COLOR Keep in mind how much color can do to personalize your living environment. This home creates a fresh color palette through the use of paint, furnishings and window treatments — all enhanced by the accents of Lindal cedar.

PORCHES AND DECKS Extend your living space outdoors with covered porches or decks. This Finnish-inspired home has a generous front porch that runs the entire length of the house. The back porch includes an outdoor shower for cooling off after relaxing in the adjacent sauna.

START *Month 1–2*
Found site and contacted Lindal dealer

PREPARATION *Month 3–4*
Plans developed by *Home* magazine, Lindal, and dealer

Month 5
Contact builder and subcontractors

Month 6
Permits obtained

INTERPRETING A FINNISH SENSE OF STYLE AND SPACE Inspired by the summer cottages she visited in Finland, editor Gale Steves envisioned a home that makes the best use of a relatively small living space — one where "every inch is lived in." Lindal's classic post and beam construction supports the open floorplan, high ceilings and custom windows that give this modest-size home its sense of spaciousness. Open to the kitchen and dining room, the great room functions as a multi-use space for entertaining and relaxing. Two bedrooms share a well-placed main-floor bath; the laundry is conveniently close to the kitchen. Upstairs, a full master suite and a home office claim the most private part of the home with a romantic, lofty feeling that comes from the high, sloped ceilings and gabled dormers. Together, the dormers and the covered front porch lend charm to the exterior and provide an alluring hint of life inside that sunny-yellow front door. **BEDROOMS** three + office **BATHROOMS** two **TOTAL AREA** 1,753 sq ft **SIZE** 42' x 33'

CHAPEL HILL
First floor

COVERED PORCH (Included)
UTIL
BEDROOM 14' x 10'
KITCHEN / 11' x 11'
DINING 11' x 11'
CL
B
CL
CL
GREAT ROOM 20' x 16'
BEDROOM 13' x 10'
CL
Up
ENTRY
COVERED PORCH (Included)

CHAPEL HILL
Second floor

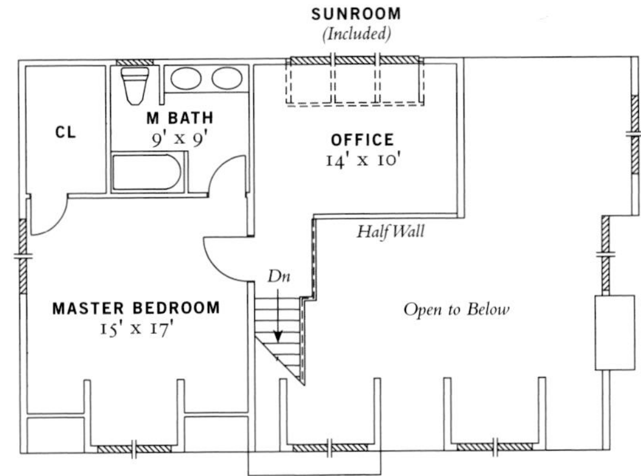

0 feet *10 feet* *20 feet*

1/16 inch represents 1 foot

BUILDING *Month 7* — Temporary power, excavation, foundation, delivery of materials

Month 8 — Floor system, beams, rafters, roof

Month 9 — Windows, siding, doors, plumbing, electrical, insulation

Month 10 — Drywall, liner, painting, cabinets, floor coverings

Month 11 — Landscaping, move in

06

Imagine coming home to a perfect curve of sandy beach. The sound of waves lapping at the shore. The shimmering of a golden sunset on the water. And a personal retreat as spectacular as its setting. For John and Sue Boyle, their lakefront Lindal home in Virginia is a retirement dream come true. Located a world away from city life, and less than two minutes from their favorite golf course, the Boyles' home is filled with natural light, water views — and a relaxed elegance in which family and friends feel very much at home.

Long before the Boyles built their custom Lindal on the lake, Sue had walked through it in her mind. Having designed three of the couple's previous homes, she said, "I knew exactly how we were going to live in the home and what was important to us." To take every advantage of their spacious lakefront lot, the Boyles envisioned open, airy spaces with water views from every room, sweeping expanses of windows, and the structural integrity to support the home's style and site — all signature strengths of Lindal design and engineering.

PREVIOUS SPREAD With its turret-flanked prow and Chippendale-style deck railing, the lake side of the Boyles' home is as polished and pretty as the front. THIS PAGE: ABOVE John and Sue Boyle at the grand entrance to their home. OPPOSITE The stone exterior of the dining room complements the natural beauty of Lindal cedar siding. Varying roof heights add interest; retaining the same roof pitch creates harmony.

"Lindal's design flexibility and ingenuity allowed us to strike the aesthetic balance we had in mind: contemporary on the outside, and more traditional inside."

"As soon as we opened the planbook, we knew Lindal was the type of home we wanted," John said. "It was clearly the way to go in terms of being able to truly customize. We also wanted to ensure that the materials going into this home were of the very best quality. With Lindal, we never had any worries about the materials not 'living up' to the home."

With Sue's detailed wish list and her preliminary hand-drawn floorplans inspired by a home in the Lindal planbook, Lindal dealer team Roland and Betty Riddick worked closely with the couple to bring their vision to life. "From the kitchen countertops to the ceiling fans, Sue knew just what she wanted, which was a joy," Roland said. "I focused on resolving the technical issues of the design, developing scaled drawings and translating the plan into Lindal's classic post and beam building system."

Many of Lindal's designs are ideal for waterfront and golf course lots, where the back of the home needs to be just as welcoming aesthetically and functionally as the front. "The wall of windows on the lake side of our house is such a statement in itself that it was easy to create the sense of two 'fronts,' " Sue said. "That's not a given in an ordinary home."

The Boyles are delighted that Lindal gave them the best of both worlds stylistically: contemporary outside, more traditional inside. The beauty of stained cedar siding enhances the contemporary look of their home's exterior. Inside, posts, beams and walls are finished with paint colors and wallpapers that complement the couple's love for traditional and antique furnishings.

A uniquely designed and engineered roof system was required to accommodate the home's graceful turrets — two romantic viewpoints rounding off each end of the home on the lake side. "We never saw the turrets as a challenge, because Roland spent a lot of time resolving all the design issues for us," John said. "We are impressed with *(continued on page 102)*

THIS PAGE: LEFT Just off the great room, the dining room glows with the natural light from a wall of windows. **RIGHT** Lindal's classic post and beam construction and engineering allow for an open flow of living space and high, angled ceilings that take on a sculptural drama. **OPPOSITE** With its two-story Lindal prow window looking out to the water, the Boyles' great room gives them easy access to some of their favorite things: their books, main stereo system and lakeside deck.

THIS PAGE: TOP A hanging box above the kitchen island uses cabinet-like panels to house the recessed lighting. **BOTTOM** The home's lake level includes a warm, cozy bar just off the family/media room. **OPPOSITE** Knowing that "everyone ends up in the kitchen," Sue Boyle planned for ample space and storage.

"With Lindal, the quality of materials going into your home is not at the builder's discretion or limited by local availability. That makes a difference you notice every day."

(continued from page 98) the way the entire ceiling system works, from the wonderfully interesting ceiling angles inside the turreted areas to the quality of the roof insulation and the cedar shakes."

Having embarked on this home with the wisdom of their past experiences, the Boyles emphasize that success is not only a matter of good design and materials, it's a matter of good relationships. Creating a custom home takes a level of collaboration, attention to detail and dependable follow-through that is not easy to find. Looking back on building their previous homes, they say they enjoyed a better level of service from their Lindal dealer than is customary with a traditional architect-builder approach.

"The Riddicks acted as our go-betweens so there were no hassles or mistakes," Sue said. "Typically, the owner has to take on some of that. Not being a builder or architect, that's quite difficult for the homeowner. But Roland took care of it all, and Lindal came through with everything. There just wasn't any hassle in building this home."

Most importantly, the relationship resulted in the realization of the couple's dream, helping them to create not just a custom home but a way of life. "Roland was able to take what Sue had in her head and put it on paper to make it real," John said. "It turned out just the way we dreamed. He solved our design and engineering problems. He found our builder. He even found us a place to stay while the house was being built."

Along the way, Sue added, Roland and his wife, Betty, became more than business associates. "They became our friends."

LINDAL CONSULTATION: *Smith Mountain Cedar Homes*
LANDSCAPE ARCHITECT: *Proctor S. Harvey & Associates*
BUILDER: *Gary Rogers, Sunrise Builders*
INTERIOR DESIGN: *Sue Boyle*

THIS PAGE: TOP Considering the deck an integral part of their home, the Boyles made it wide enough to function as a true outdoor room for barbecuing and entertaining. **BOTTOM** John and Sue with their dealers, Roland and Betty Riddick. **OPPOSITE** Every step of the way, the Boyles took their waterfront site into consideration, creating a dock, boathouse and lakeshore landscaping that feel right at home.

BATHROOMS Think about comfort and resale value when you plan your bathrooms. The Boyles' spacious master bath includes a double-sink vanity, a true whirlpool tub (the therapeutic difference is significant, they emphasize) and a separate, oversized shower with a 17-inch-high, built-in seat.

LIVE IN IT Sue Boyle can't emphasize it enough: Before you design your new home, "live" in it in your mind. Think through how you'll use your home and where you'll entertain guests. Visualize everything from the big issues — the flow between rooms and how you'll access outdoor areas — to smaller but important planning details like wiring for phones, lighting and electronics.

POST AND BEAM SYSTEM Take advantage of Lindal's classic post and beam building system to create a gentle flow from room to room by using wide entrances instead of narrow doorways. Not only does this create a gracious sense of spaciousness and ease — it can enhance your home's value.

SEPARATE SPACES Consider ways to separate the quiet, private spaces of your home from the more public areas you'll share with guests. The Boyles clearly defined welcoming spaces for family and friends — and private places where, as Sue puts it, "it's just John and me."

KITCHENS Don't skimp on the size of your kitchen or the amount of space needed to store things out of sight, Sue suggests. "If everyone ends up in your kitchen the way they do in ours, you'll want plenty of both."

DECKS Right from the start, think of your deck as an extension of your home's living space. Easy access to all major main-level rooms and a pristine Chippendale-style railing make the Boyles' deck a charming al fresco space for dining and entertaining almost year round.

START *Month 1*
Found site and contacted Lindal dealer

PREPARATION *Month 2–10*
Plans developed by homeowner and Lindal

Month 8
Financing arranged, contractors selected

Month 11–12
Permits obtained, temporary power, excavation, foundation, first delivery of materials

AT HOME ON THE WATER The Boyles began their planning process by "thinking outside the box," confident that Lindal's classic post and beam construction would support a 26-foot-high great room ceiling, 84 windowpanes to look west over the lake — and even a turret or two. Outside, the architectural and landscaping design gives the home two "fronts"; the face it presents to the lake is as inviting as the street front. Dramatic turrets and rooflines were conceptualized by Sue Boyle, engineered by Lindal. Inside, the open flow of large rooms and high ceilings maximizes lake views and natural light on both living levels. The main level, with its luxurious master suite, is designed around the owners' lives and love of entertaining. Downstairs, the lake level has the amenities and privacy of a separate guest suite on the water for family and friends. The lakeside deck is an outdoor living space that runs the entire length of the home and is accessible from every major room on the main floor. BEDROOMS three + office BATHROOMS two + one three-quarter + two half TOTAL AREA 6,522 sq ft SIZE 150' x 64'

LAKEFRONT LIVING
First floor

LAKEFRONT LIVING
Daylight basement

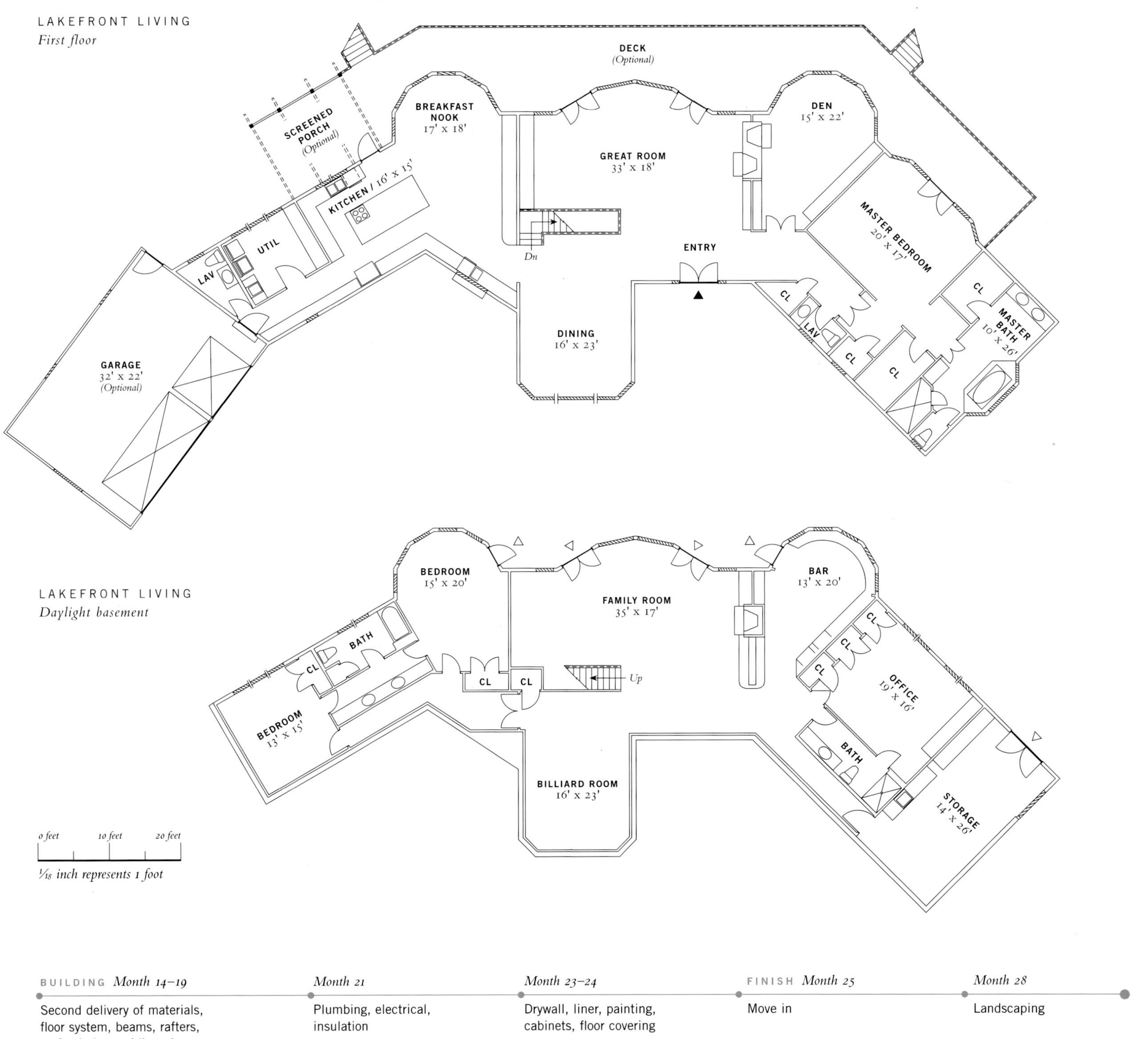

BUILDING *Month 14–19*
Second delivery of materials, floor system, beams, rafters, roof, windows, siding, doors

Month 21
Plumbing, electrical, insulation

Month 23–24
Drywall, liner, painting, cabinets, floor covering

FINISH *Month 25*
Move in

Month 28
Landscaping

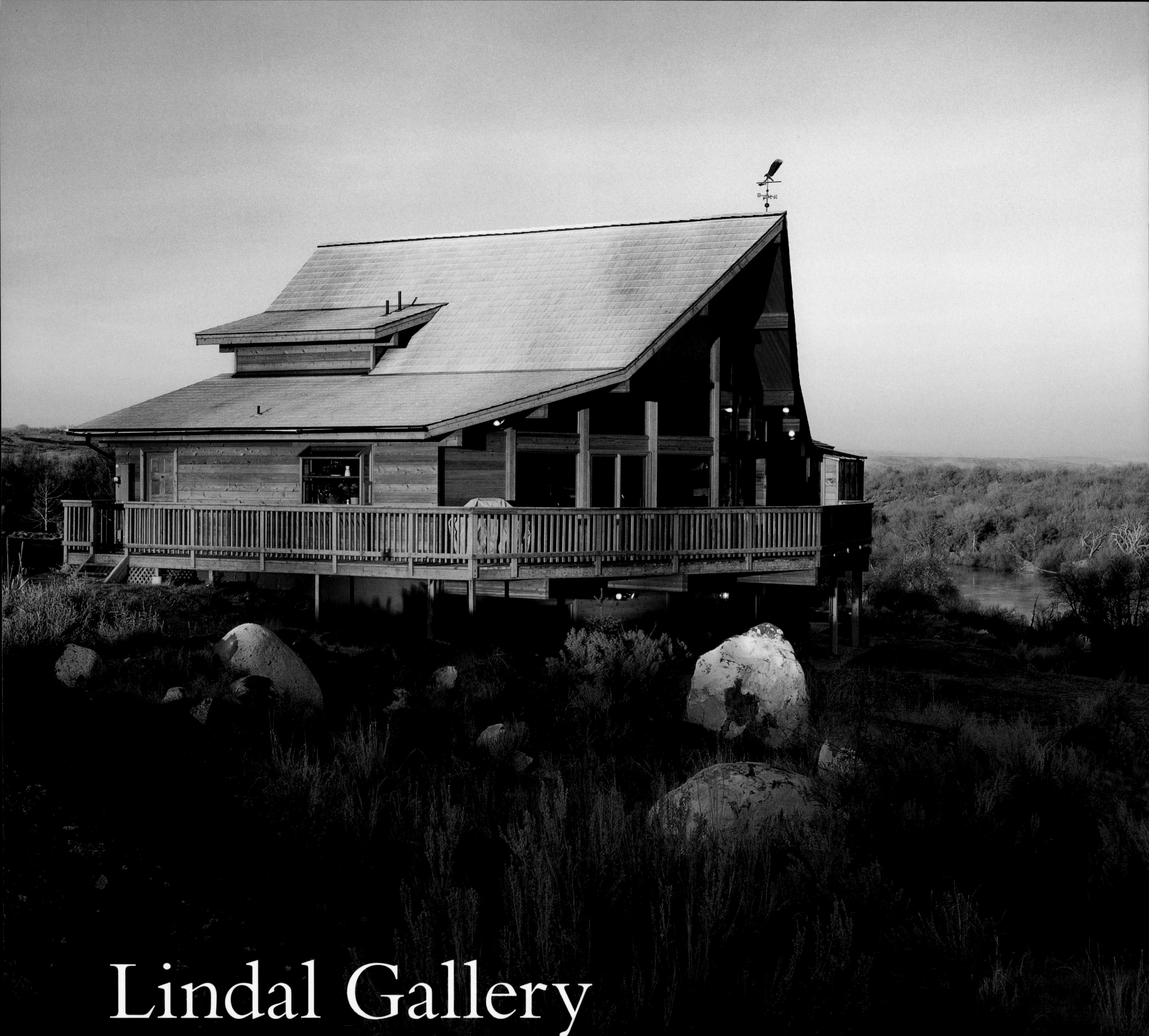

Lindal Gallery

Now that you've seen how six Lindal homeowners brought their dreams to life, this next home tour is dedicated to yours. Start with the overall look and feel you want — the style of your home. Is it a Classic Lindal that captures your view with a two-story prow of windows? A Traditional Lindal with the architectural lineage of a farmhouse, a Tudor or a Colonial? Or a Contemporary Lindal, a masterpiece of clean lines and modern livability? Browse through the photographs in our Gallery and get acquainted with the elements of style that speak to you. Then let us help you bring them home.

PREVIOUS SPREAD The large prow and clapboard cedar siding of this popular Summit plan are characteristic of Classic Lindal designs. Weinert/Jordan residence, ID. Customized Summit. **OPPOSITE** This Lindal was created for its own island. Gluek residence, Ontario. Customized Prow Star. **THIS PAGE** The flexibility of Classic Lindal design allows for a wide range of variations: daylight basements, main-floor wings on one or both sides of the prow, and accent materials from brick to metal roofs. Stained cedar siding is a popular exterior look; it allows the beauty of Lindal cedar to shine through. 1. Anderson residence, IL. Customized Chalet Star 2. Babich residence, WA. Customized Prow Star. 3. McDonald residence, NV. Customized Meadowbrook plan. Ⓟ 77 4. Pacific National Exhibition, BC. Customized Prow Star. 5. Porter residence, Ontario. Customized Contempo Prow Star. 6. Trocino/Marx residence, NY. Custom home.

OPPOSITE: 1. This North Carolina home combines cedar siding, stucco accents and a tile roof. Digh residence, NC. Casa Islena plan. ⓟ 67. **BOTTOM** Three stunning examples of how artfully Classic Lindals enhance a variety of building sites. 2. Moeller residence, CA. Customized Prow Star. 3. Osato Research Institute, Japan. Customized Casa Islena. 4. A daylight basement is a cost-efficient way to add more square feet. Schlieff residence, MA. Customized Countryside. **THIS PAGE** This view home combines solid-cedar construction with Classic Lindal design. Smith residence, ID. Customized Prow Star.

THIS PAGE: 1. The signature prow of Classic Lindal design creates a wall of windows that follows the height of the roofline — letting in natural light and your favorite view. Fiese residence, NY. Customized Contempo Prow Star. 2. Anderson residence, IL. Customized Chalet Star. 3. Harlan residence, MT. Custom home. 4. South residence, NJ. Customized Panorama. **OPPOSITE:** Whether you love the rustic beauty of exposed beams and a stone fireplace, the look of an open loft or the elegance of antique furnishings, you can have it all in a Classic Lindal — including, of course, your view. 5. Wiking residence, ID. Customized Casa. 6. McDonald residence, NV. Customized Meadowbrook plan. Ⓟ 77 7. Stout residence, OR. Customized Prow. 8. Vaucher residence, OR. Customized Contempo Prow Star.

5

6

7

8

1

2

3

4

OPPOSITE The ultimate log home. Crafted of 4-by-8 inch solid cedar timbers, this Contemporary Lindal cuts a sculptural profile against a backdrop of mountains in Montana. Osborn residence, MT. Custom home. **THIS PAGE** Contemporary Lindal designs are at home anywhere — from California ski country (top left) to Japan (bottom right). 1. Disbrow residence, CA. Custom home. 2. Bohnenberger residence, SC. Custom home. 3. Coleman residence, SC. Customized Signature. 4. Suzuki residence, Japan. Customized Liberty.

THIS PAGE The lake side appeal of this Contemporary is enhanced by a mix of roof heights, window shapes and the light-gray vertical cedar siding. Hodgkinson residence, Ontario. Customized Ellington plan. Ⓟ 107. **OPPOSITE: 1.** Even from the outside, the livability of this gray-stained clapboard Lindal comes through in its balcony off the master bedroom, the sunroom off the kitchen and the French doors off the dining room. Newsome residence, VT. Customized Arbor Place plan. Ⓟ 98. **2.** Skylights are a popular addition to Contemporary Lindals. Pacific National Exhibition, BC. Custom home **3.** Stained cedar siding and a tile roof weather the elements of a tropical setting beautifully. Karahalios residence, HI. Custom home.

THIS PAGE: 1. Palladian windows grace the contemporary prow of this Lindal. Hodgkinson residence, Ontario. Customized Ellington plan. Ⓟ 107. 2. High ceilings and fine cabinetry make for an elegant kitchen. Harlan residence, MT. Custom home. 3. Contemporary Lindal design accommodates a traditional Japanese tatami room. Yamadai Housing Company, Japan. Custom home. 4. Bleached and stained wood increases the light, airy effect of the astral windows in this Contemporary Lindal kitchen. Gilman residence, CA. Customized Contempo Prow Star. **OPPOSITE** Contemporary Lindals can be furnished with modern decor, traditional flourishes or aesthetic contrasts such as the clawfoot tub and the lacy-looking four-poster. 5. Disbrow residence, CA. Custom home. 6. Gassner residence, OR. Octagon Oasis plan. Ⓟ 110. 7. Hurlbutt residence, ID. Custom Pole. 8. Sheppard residence, SC. Custom home.

5

7

6

8

1

2

3

4

OPPOSITE: Traditional Lindal designs are a favorite from snowy settings to the cottage country of Canada; deep overhangs and spacious porches are popular everywhere. **1.** Dixon residence, MT. Customized Chapel Hill. **2.** Johnson residence, IL. Custom home. **3.** Wolfe residence, CA. Custom home. **4.** Custom residence, Ontario. Customized Muskoka. **THIS PAGE** The beauty of Traditional Lindals is in their architectural detail, from gabled dormers and gambrel roofs to clapboard siding and tropical pole-house design. **5.** Custom residence, WA. Customized Cape Breton. **6.** Burnop residence, VA. Custom home. **7.** Mock residence, PA. Custom home. **8.** Suhs residence, MI. Custom home. **9.** Harrington residence, HI. Customized Pole.

5

6

7

8

9

1

2

3

4

THIS PAGE Traditional Lindals offer an untraditional sense of open, airy spaciousness throughout the interior. 1. Coleman residence, SC. Customized Signature. 2. Custom residence, CA. Casa Carolina plan. P 65. 3. Gary Ksander & Gail Denemark residence, NJ. Prow Star: Lake Vista plan. P 89. 4. Custom residence, CA. Casa Carolina plan. P 65. **OPPOSITE:** 5. Two quarter-round windows top the double swinging patio doors and cedar trim complements the brick fireplace in this living room. Suhs residence, MI. Custom home. 6. The owners chose optional peeled logs for the support posts of their ski retreat. Wolfe residence, CA. Custom home. 7. Cedar ceiling liner complements the mix of traditional and antique furnishings. Mock residence, PA. Custom home. 8. A pine ceiling and exposed beams add rustic appeal to a cozy kitchen. Suhs residence, MI. Custom home.

Bungalow Palani
BUNGALOW SERIES | Simpler times come to mind with the large covered porch of the quaint Bungalow Palani. A breakfast bar off the kitchen provides a convenient area for conversing with friends and family. Located in the back of the house, the master bedroom with its own private deck creates a relaxing refuge after a busy day.
Lindal

Now that you've explored the world of *Lindal Living*, the excitement is really just beginning. *Lindal Planning* is our 144-page guide brimming with the best of Lindal plans, advice and inspiration for creating your new home. Gather your family around the table for the fun of answering the Lifestyle Inventory as you focus on the elements of design and style that matter most to you. Take an armchair tour of the latest, greatest home plans from the extensive Lindal design library. And gain hundreds of useful tips from Lindal's design experts on every aspect of planning your new home.

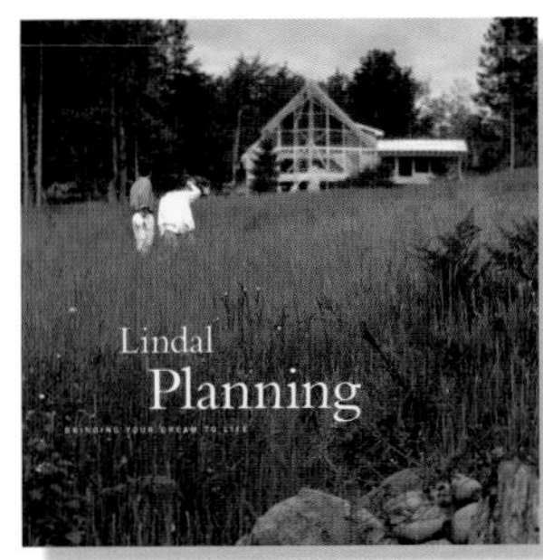

Of course, there's nothing like experiencing Lindal style and quality firsthand — at your local Lindal dealer. Your Lindal dealer can answer any preliminary questions you have, from plan modifications and budget to local building codes and site considerations. And when you're ready, no one is better able to help you transform your wish list into the best of plans.

At Lindal, we've been helping people live their dreams for more than half a century. We look forward to doing the same for you. For the name and location of your nearest local independent Lindal dealer, simply call us toll-free at 1.800.426.0536 or visit Lindal on the Web at: http://www.lindal.com.

Index by Subject

Index of Photography